Praise for Merrill Markoe
What the Dogs Have Taught Me

"Merrill Markoe has a keen eye for the little lunacies of modern living. . . . Hers is a special talent, desperately needed these days."
—*The New York Times*

"You will gain an appreciation of the silly from which you may never recover. You may begin to collect windup toys at airports, catalogs of exotic nightwear, and unemployment ads for stun-gun salesmen."
—*Time*

How to Be Hap- Hap- Happy Like Me

"Markoe is the funniest woman in America and, please, let's have no arguing, okay?"
—*People*

"Hip, hilarious, a neurotic's delight . . . Markoe presents a stupefyingly funny guide to the universe and everything in it."
—*The Houston Post*

What the Dogs Have Taught Me

Merrill Markoe

·

What the Dogs Have Taught Me

·

And Other Amazing Things I've Learned

VILLARD
NEW YORK

To Stan, Bob, Bo, Tex,

Winky, Dinky, and Puppyboy,

but most of all to Lewis

Foreword

On the eve of the republication of this book of short pieces, I cannot help but reflect on how much has changed since the nineties, when many of them were written.

Back then I was single, and coping with dating, while living with my four head of dog in an underfurnished house in Los Angeles. I was cynical about the importance of the Internet or the need for e-mail, and scared silly about the frightening specter of El Niño, the unstoppable Ebola virus, skyrocketing electricity prices and the nightmare of rolling blackouts, the coming catastrophe of Y2K, the crazy war in Kuwait, and the number of fat grams I was consuming each day. I was also worried sick about the cavalier destruction of the environment, the rising censorship by the religious right, the lack of regard the current administration was showing for the truth, and the puzzling desire for a return of the seventies. Some things don't change.

Now it is 2005. I am coping with living with one head of man, and two head of dog and cat in the same house in Los Angeles, but has become overfurnished. Now I am cynical about the need for a cell phone that is also a camera, and scared silly about skyrocketing gas prices, the specter of the worst fire season ever, the unstoppable West Nile virus, the crazy war in Iraq, and the number of carbs I am consuming each day.

On the bright side, all this time I have continued to learn from my dogs, who have always been there to make life look like a hopeful, happy place. They have taught me, by example, that it is possible to wake up each morning in a wonderful mood, worried about absolutely nothing, excited about breakfast, thrilled every time there is a knock at the door. How can I ever forget the reaction they had to the last big fire scare in my neighborhood, when the fire department came to my house to suggest we evacuate? While I was frantic, running around trying to determine which of my possessions to save, the dogs all were leaping with glee at the prospect of some kind of event that was going to involve not just leashes but also the car.

Through constant and ceaseless example, the dogs have taught me that this bottomless joie de vivre is available to each and every one of us. All it takes is someone looking out for your health and your grooming while serving you nutritious meals plus vitamins every day as they selflessly make sure you get plenty of exercise and love and comfort. It also helps if they pay all of your bills.

Since I have had no one to rely on for those things since high school, I have been a nervous wreck for decades.

But my dogs are always the picture of health and happiness. And isn't that what's really important?

MERRILL MARKOE

Contents

Contents

Contents

What the Dogs Have Taught Me

A Conversation
with My Dogs

It is late afternoon. Seated at my desk, I call for my dogs to join me in my office. They do.

> *Me:* The reason I've summoned you here today is I really think we should talk about something.
>
> *Bob:* What's that?
>
> *Me:* Well, please don't take this the wrong way, but I get the feeling you guys think you *have* to follow me *everywhere* and I just want you both to know that you don't.
>
> *Stan:* Where would you get a feeling like that?
>
> *Me:* I get it from the fact that the both of you follow me *everywhere* all day long. Like for instance, this morning. We were all together in the bedroom? Why do you both look blank? Doesn't this ring a bell at all? I was on the bed reading the paper . . .
>
> *Bob:* Where was I?
>
> *Me:* On the floor sleeping.

Bob: On the floor sleepi . . . ? Oh, yes. Right. I remember that. Go on.

Me: So, there came a point where I had to get up and go into the next room to get a Kleenex. And you *both* woke up out of a deep sleep to go with me.

Stan: Yes. So? What's the problem?

Bob: We *like* to watch you get Kleenex. We happen to think it's something you do very well.

Me: The point I'm trying to make is why do you both have to get up out of a deep sleep to go *with* me. You sit there staring at me, all excited, like you think something really good is going to happen. I feel a lot of pressure to be more entertaining.

Bob: Would it help if we stood?

Stan: I think what the lady is saying is that where Kleenex retrieval is concerned, she'd just as soon we not make the trip.

Bob: Is that true?

Me: Yes. It is.

Bob (deeply hurt): Oh, man.

Stan: Don't let her get to you, buddy.

Bob: I know I shouldn't. But it all comes as such a shock.

Me: I think you may be taking this wrong. It's not that I don't like your company. It's just that I see no reason for you both to follow me every time I get up.

Bob: What if just one of us goes?

Stan: And I don't suppose that "one of us" would be *you?*

Me: *Neither* of you needs to go.

Bob: Okay. Fine. No problem. Get your damn Kleenex alone from now on.

Me: Good.

Bob: I'm just curious. What's your position on pens?

Me: Pens?

Bob: Yes. How many of us can wake up out of a deep sleep to watch you look for a pen?

Me: Why would *either* of you want to wake up out of a deep sleep to follow me around while I'm looking for a pen?

Stan: Is she serious?

Bob: I can't tell. She has such a weird sense of humor.

Me: Let's just level with each other, okay? The *real* reason you both follow me every place I go is that you secretly believe there might be food involved. Isn't that true? Isn't that the real reason for the show of enthusiasm?

Stan: Very nice talk.

Bob: The woman has got some mouth on her.

Me: You mean you *deny* that every time you follow me out of the room it's actually because you think we're stopping for snacks?

Bob: Absolutely false. That is a bald-faced lie. We do it for the life experience. Period.

Stan: And sometimes I think it might work into a game of ball.

Bob: But we certainly don't *expect* anything.

Stan: We're *way* past expecting anything of you. We wouldn't want you to overexert yourself in any way. You have to rest and save up all your strength for all that Kleenex fetching.

Bob: Plus we know it doesn't concern you in the least that we're both *starving to death*.

Stan: We consume on the average about a third of the calories eaten daily by the typical wasted South American street dog.

Me: *One* bowl of food a day is what the *vet* said I should give you. No more.

Bob: One bowl of food is a joke. It's an hors d'oeuvre. It does nothing but whet my appetite.

Me: Last summer, before I cut your food down, you were the size and shape of a hassock.

Bob: Who is she talking to?

Stan: You, pal. You looked like a beanbag chair, buddy.

Bob: But it was not from overeating. In summer, I retain fluids, that's all. I was in very good shape.

Stan: For a hippo. I saw you play ball back then. Nice energy. For a dead guy.

Bob: Don't talk to me about energy. Who single-handedly ate his way through the back fence? Not just once but on *four separate occasions*?

Me: So *you're* the one who did that?

Bob: One who did what?

Me: Ate through the back fence.

Bob: Is there something wrong with the back fence? I have no idea what happened. Whoever said that is a liar.

Stan: The fact remains that we are starving all day long and you continually torture us by eating right in front of us.

Bob: Very nice manners, by the way.

Me: You have the nerve to discuss my manners? Who drinks out of the toilet and then comes up and kisses me on the face?

Bob: That would be Dave.

Me: No. That would be *you*. And while we're on the subject of manners, who keeps trying to crawl *into* the refrigerator? Who always has *mud* on their tongue?

Stan: Well, that would be Dave.

Me: Okay. That *would* be Dave. But the point I'm trying to make is that where manners are concerned, let's just say that you don't catch me trying to stick my head in *your* dinner.

Bob: Well, that may be more a function of menu than anything else.

Me: Which brings me right back to my original point. The two of you do not have to wake up and offer me fake camaraderie now that you understand that *once* a day is all you're ever going to be fed. Period. Non-negotiable. For the rest of your natural lives. And if I want to play ball, I'll *say so*. End of sentence.

Stan: Well, I see that the nature of these talks has completely broken down.

Bob: I gotta tell you, it hurts.

Me: There's no reason to have hurt feelings.

Stan: Fine. Whatever you say.

Bob: I just don't give a damn anymore. I'm beyond that, quite frankly. Get your own Kleenex, for all I care.

Stan: I feel the same way. Let her go get all the Kleenex and pens she wants. I couldn't care less.

Me: Excellent. Well, I hope we understand each other now.

Bob: We do. Why'd you get up? Where are you going?

Me: Into the next room.

Stan: Oh. Mm hmm. I see. And why is that?

Me: To get my purse.

Stan: Hey, fatso, out of my way.

Bob: Watch out, asshole. I was first.

Stan: The hell you were. *I* was first.

Bob: Fuck you. We're getting her purse, I go first. I'm *starving*.

Stan: You don't listen at all, do you. Going for *pens* means food. She said she's getting her *purse*. That means *ball*.

Just Say "I Do"

I've been giving a lot of thought to the idea of getting married lately. Ever since President Bush decided to go out on a limb and give "marriage" his ringing endorsement, thereby proposing another forward-thinking political initiative on behalf of the Republican party that may at long last lay the groundwork for a full slate of all the other things your mother always told you to do, such as getting the hair out of your eyes, standing up straight, changing your tone of voice when you talk to me, and not leaving the house looking like that.

Bush's real agenda, of course, is to address the considerable pressure being applied by conservative religious organizations to back a constitutional amendment banning same-sex marriage. Opponents of same-sex marriage like to cite the ability to have children as the significant line of demarcation between a real marriage and a fraudulent same-sex facsimile. However, in making this case, they conveniently forget to mention some of "real marriage"'s famous offspring—for example, Adolf

Hitler, Jeffrey Dahmer, the Enron guys, and the terrorists who engineered 9/11.

Statistically speaking, gay marriage stands alone as the last outpost of marriage's most pristine ideals, since same-sex couples are the only ones whose marital track records are untarnished. If we are going to question the validity of these marriages, then that proposed constitutional amendment ought to also contain a subclause restricting certain heterosexual unions that have, in the fullness of time, proven to be totally futile. For instance, the marriages of movie stars to anyone, straight or gay, especially if they have participated in a *People* magazine article in which they have declared that they are "very much in love." Or weddings involving people under twenty-eight who have known each other for less than a year and intend to say their vows while wearing a parachute, scuba gear, or anything else that celebrates their hobbies.

In fact, when you look at the big picture, it is easy to conclude that the best thing for our culture might be to just give marriage to gay people and let them refurbish it the way they do run-down neighborhoods. Once they have restored it to its original authentic beauty, plus added all the modern upgrades, heterosexuals can be permitted to return to it and continue their pattern of systematic debasement.

But here's the part about the whole issue of who can get married and who cannot that really has me puzzled. Back in February, when San Francisco mayor Gavin Newsom started issuing marriage licenses to same-sex partners, 3,000 gay couples rushed to the altar. That's *6,000* adults who couldn't wait another minute for the opportunity to be eligible to sue each other over common property, pay alimony, and take out mutual restraining orders. And that's what I found unsettling.

Not because the idea of gay marriage gives me pause, but precisely because the only marriage I seem to have a real problem with is my own. As a certified straight person (and yes, I did take the trouble to become certified), I have been legally entitled to get married for over four decades. Yet never once have I been able to motivate myself sufficiently to push a relationship further in that direction. Although I have been much live-togethered, I have never walked down an aisle that doesn't have something I need that is on sale.

It isn't because I haven't had access to successful relationships. For the past three years, I have been in a really good one, perhaps my best ever. In it, not only have I learned to talk through disagreements instead of driving around for hours in my car with a packed suitcase, but have gazed with astonishment at my partner as he actually listened when I talked. I even have proof: I have given him a number of pop quizzes. And still I remain the quiet calm spot in a tornado of peer group weddings, the only person who has never made all her friends shell out money to buy her china and silver and matching flatware and therefore does not yet have any of the aforementioned and is frankly a little pissed off about the whole thing. Especially when I add it all up and realize I have paid for so many sets of other people's pricey wedding-registry china that I could easily host a dinner for the entire State Department if I could stand to be in their presence.

Oh, sure, the first guy I lived with played the marriage card during our breakup, in one of those desperate eleventh-inning maneuvers that I never fall for because they remind me of nothing so much as an evening of avant-garde theater. And the next guy and I actually once went and had premarital blood tests. But I think it was because he just liked going to the doctor. In his perfect world, a marriage license would also have required a brain scan, an electrocardiogram, and a sphygmomanometer reading.

The key point here is that it wasn't as if I were the poor little wan and weeping thing who was left at the altar, or the frail victim of heartless commitment-phobic womanizers. Although, of course, I have enjoyed the company of such men on many delightful occasions. No, I had no intention of ever marrying any of the guys I have loved. I've never even had a fantasy about how my wedding would be. Occasionally I would want the men who claimed to love me to say that they would like to marry me, but that was really an exercise in positive reinforcement, like when you make someone tell you over and over they don't think you look fat.

When my father was dying, I asked him what he considered the biggest success in his life. When, without hesitation, he answered, "My marriage," it made me wonder for a moment if he was a closet polygamist. Because the marriage I saw him in was one that sounded like this: "I *said* I love you. Now what the hell else do you *want* from me, for Chrissakes?"

On a related topic, not long ago I was reading through my childhood diaries and I found that as early as fifth grade I wrote, "I am never getting married. I am never having kids." Of course, a couple of pages later I also wrote, "I am never having my period." Apparently I had the foresight to rethink that one.

So why, then, when I attended someone's wedding recently and the bride threw the bouquet to me, did I turn and duck so it bounced off my shoulder? Why does the idea of announcing to the world in a ceremony that you belong to someone and they to you, forever and ever, give me the feeling that I am tied to a chair in a windowless room, unable to reach the phone to find the number of Rush Limbaugh's doctor and beg him to prescribe me some of that OxyContin? The craziest part of it all is that I like the idea of being in a monogamous relationship with someone I love. And when I'm in one, I do my best to make the object of my affections happy. I have even been known to take a Vivarin at midnight in order to cook and serve dinner at three A.M., when my beloved shows up and is hungry.

Which is why I find myself wondering: What do those 6,000 gay people in San Francisco have in their hearts that I don't have in mine, besides an obsession with Barbra Streisand? What do they and all the much married people of America all know about love that I have yet to comprehend?

But then, as soon as I find myself getting wrapped up in romanticizing, I begin to think: If other people have so much more emotional depth than I do, why are there so many marriages that last only a few months? Or marriages where the sex has been dead for decades? Why is there so much cheating and complaining, so many vile divorce-related postmarital lawsuits where both people are trying not only to rob each other of everything they own, but also to impose stiff penalties for having been stupid enough to agree to the marriage in the first place? Why are there women who marry one violence-prone alcoholic, or drug addict, or pedophile after another? What rational justification can there be for the marital track records of an Elizabeth Taylor or a Liza Minnelli? And when I think about all that, I wind up right back where I started.

Which brings me to the only solution to my dilemma that I can think of. If I could get George Bush and his band of goofballs to pass a constitutional amendment prohibiting *me* from getting married, I feel fairly certain there would be nothing that could keep me from insisting on getting married as soon as possible. Suddenly, like all those marriage-hungry couples of the gay community, I would find there was nothing I could imagine wanting more.

The Dog Diaries

I pick dogs that remind me of myself—scrappy, mutt-faced, with a hint of mange. People look for a reflection of their own personalities or the person they dream of being in the eyes of an animal companion. That is the reason I sometimes look into the face of my dog Stan and see wistful sadness and existential angst, when all he is actually doing is slowly scanning the ceiling for flies.

We pet owners demand a great deal from our pets. When we give them the job, it's a career position. Pets are required to listen to us blithely, even if we talk to them in infantile and goofy tones of voice that we'd never dare use around another human being for fear of being forced into psychiatric observation. On top of that, we make them wear little sweaters or jackets, and not just the cool kind with the push-up sleeves, either, but weird little felt ones that say IT'S RAINING CATS AND DOGS.

We are pretty sure that we and our pets share the same reality, until one day we come home to find that our wistful, intelligent friend who reminds us of our better self has decided a good way to spend the day is to open a box of Brillo pads, unravel a few, distribute some throughout the house, and eat or wear all the rest. And we shake our heads in inability to comprehend what went wrong here.

Is he bored or is he just out for revenge? He certainly can't be as stupid as this would indicate. In order to answer these questions more fully, I felt I needed some kind of new perspective, a perspective that comes from really knowing both sides of the story.

Thus, I made up my mind to live with my pets as one of them: to share their hopes, their fears, their squeaking vinyl lamb chops, their drinking space at the toilet.

What follows is the revealing, sometimes shocking, sometimes terrifying, sometimes really stupid diary that resulted.

8:45 A.M. We have been lying on our sides in the kitchen for almost an hour now. We started out in the bedroom with just our heads under the bed. But then one of us heard something, and we all ran to the back door. I think our quick response was rather effective because, although I never ascertained exactly what we heard to begin with, I also can't say I recall ever hearing it again.

9:00 A.M. We carefully inspected the molding in the hallway, which led us straight to the heating duct by the bedroom. Just a coincidence? None of us was really sure. So we watched it suspiciously for a while. Then we watched it for a little while longer.

Then, never letting it out of our sight, we all took a nap.

10:00 A.M. I don't really know whose idea it was to yank

back the edge of the carpet and pull apart the carpet pad, but talk about a rousing good time! How strange that I could have lived in this house for all these years, and never before felt the fur of a carpet between my teeth. Or actually bit into a moist, chewy chunk of carpet padding. I will never again think of the carpet as simply a covering for the floor.

11:15 A.M. When we all wound up in the kitchen, the other two began to stare at me eagerly. Their meaning was clear. The pressure was on for me to produce snacks. They remembered the old me—the one with the opposable thumb, the one who could open refrigerators and cabinets. I saw they didn't yet realize that today, I intended to live as their equal. But as they continued their staring, I soon became caught up in their obsession. That is the only explanation I have as to why I helped them topple over the garbage. At first I was nervous, watching the murky fluids soak into the floor. But the heady sense of acceptance I felt when we all dove headfirst into the can more than made up for my compromised sense of right and wrong. Pack etiquette demanded that I be the last in line. By the time I really got my head in there, the really good stuff was gone. But wait! I spied a tiny piece of tinfoil hidden in a giant clump of hair, and inside, a wad of previously chewed gum, lightly coated with sugar or salt. I was settling down to my treasure when I had the sense that I was being watched. Raising my head just slightly, I looked into the noses of my companions. Their eyes were glued to that hard rubbery mass. Their drools were long and elastic, and so, succumbing to peer pressure, I split up my gum wad three ways. But I am not sure that I did the right thing. As is so often the case with wanting popularity, I may have gained their short-term acceptance. But I think that in the long run, I lost their real respect. No dog of reasonable intelligence would ever divide up something that could still be chewed.

11:50 A.M. Someone spotted a fly, and all three of us decided to catch him in our teeth. I was greatly relieved when one of the others got to him first.

12:20 P.M. Someone heard something, and in a flash, we were all in the backyard, running back and forth by the fence, periodically hooting. Then one of us spotted a larger-than-usual space between two of the fence boards, and using both teeth and nails, began to make the space larger. Pretty soon, all three of us were doing everything in our power to help. This was a case where the old opposable thumb really came in handy. Grabbing hold of one of the splinters, I was able to enlarge the hole immediately. Ironically, I alone was unable to squeeze through to freedom, and so I watched with envy as the others ran in pointless circles in the lot next door. What was I going to do? All of my choices were difficult. Sure, I could go back into the house and get a hacksaw, or I could simply let myself out the back gate, but if I did that, did I not betray my companions? And would I not then be obligated to round us all up and punish us? No, I was a collaborator, and I had the lip splinters to prove it. So I went back to the hole and continued chewing. Only a few hundred dollars' worth of fence damage later, I was able to squeeze through that darn hole myself.

1:30 P.M. The extra time I took was just enough for me to lose sight of my two companions. And so, for the first time, I had to rely on my keen new animal instincts. Like the wild creature I had become, I was able to spot their tracks immediately. They led me in a series of ever-widening circles, then across the lot at a forty-five-degree angle, then into a series of zigzags, then back to the hole again. Finally, I decided to abandon the tracking and head out to the sidewalk. Seconds later, I spotted them both across the street, where they were racing up and back in front of the neighbor's house. They seemed glad to see me, and so I eagerly joined them in their project. The three of us had only been running and hooting for less than an hour when the apparent owner of the house came to the front door. And while I admit this may not have been the best of circumstances for a first introduction, nevertheless I still feel the manner in which he threatened to turn the hose on us was both excessively violent and unnecessarily vulgar.

Clearly, it was up to me to encourage our group to relocate, and I was shocked at how easily I could still take command of our unit. A simple "Let's go, boys," and everyone was willing to follow me home. (It's such a power-packed phrase. That's how I met my last boyfriend!)

3:00 P.M. By the time we had moved our running and hooting activities into our own front yard, we were all getting a little tired. So we lay down on our sides on the porch.

4:10 P.M. We all changed sides.

4:45 P.M. We all changed sides again.

5:20 P.M. We all lay on our backs. (What a nice change of pace!)

6:00 P.M. Everyone was starting to grow restless. Occasionally, one of us would get up, scratch the front door, and moan. I wrestled silently with the temptation simply to let us all in. But then I realized I didn't have any keys on me. Of course, it occurred to me that we could all go back through the new hole in the fence, but everyone else seemed to have forgotten about the entire fence incident by this time. As they say, "a word to the wise." And so, taking a hint from my friends, I began to forget about the whole thing myself.

6:30 P.M. The sound of an approaching car as it pulls into the driveway. The man who shares this house with us is coming home. He is both surprised and perplexed to see us all out in the front yard running in circles. He is also quickly irritated by the fact that no one offers any explanations. And once he opens the front door, he unleashes a furious string of harsh words as he confronts the mounds of garbage someone has strewn all over the house. We have nothing but sympathy for him in his tragic misfortune. But since none of us knows anything about it, we all retire to the coat closet until the whole thing blows over. And later, as he eats his dinner, I sit quietly under the table. As I watch him, a pleasant feeling of calm overtakes me as I realize just how much I have grown as a person. Perhaps that is why the cruel things he says to me seem to have no effect. And so, when he gets up to pour himself another beverage, I raise my head up to his plate, and, with my teeth, I lift off his sandwich.

Let's Party

About once a year it occurs to me that I owe a lot of people a social debt and really ought to have some kind of a party to try and pay them back. I'm not saying I *act* on this impulse. I'm just saying it occurs to me. And when it does, it is followed immediately by a sense of panic that makes me feel like one of the members of that Chilean soccer team that survived an air crash and had to contemplate eating a former teammate. In other words, I freak. The next thing I do is begin paging compulsively through books on the subject of "entertaining at home."

Of all the volumes in print on this topic, none fill me to overflowing with as much simultaneous loathing and secret envy as the combined oeuvres of Martha Stewart. Each one of these intimidating tomes is expensively bound and bursting with many, many beautiful color photographs featuring captions such as "a dramatic croquembouche surrounded by fresh flowers makes a spectacular centerpiece on the table in the library" or "Hepplewhite chairs, grandmother's plates, old silver, and long-stemmed Italian poppies grace the dining table set on our porch."

The author is a pretty blond woman with good bone structure and an uncanny ability to make whoever is her closest competitor for the title of Little Miss Perfect appear to have a learning disability. Her chapters have titles such as "Cocktails for 50—a Festive Occasion!" or "Summer Omelette Brunch Outdoors for 60!" I didn't even scan that one, since it is nearly impossible for me to get even one omelette out of a pan not looking like something I found at the bottom of my purse. But these are not the kinds of problems that plague Martha Stewart. "I always have baskets everywhere filled with fresh eggs," she tells us, perhaps while relaxing on the veranda of one of her summer homes in the mountain region of Neptune where I believe she spends a good deal of her time. Why? Because she simply gathers "eggs of all shapes, sizes, and hues from our Turkey Hill hens." She *has* her own hens. She has her own bees. She probably has a trout stream and a cranberry bog. She's always somewhere picturesque ladling something steaming into something gleaming.

The most pernicious thing about her is the way she makes the thing she recommends appear somehow vaguely doable. "To entertain at home is both a relief and a rediscovery," she says offhandedly, perhaps while seated pertly in the spacious living room of her weekend place on one of the moons of Jupiter. "It provides a good excuse to put things in order. Polish your silver. Wash forgotten dishes. Wax floors. Paint a flaking window sill." Of course it does. Especially during those long Jupiterian winters that I understand can go on for decades. *Nothing* puts *me* less in the mood for thankless chores than the swelling sense of panic that comes from planning a party.

So here at last is advice for people such as myself, busy, frazzled, with no innate hosting abilities or graces.

Merrill Markoe's Home Entertaining Guide for the Panicky Social Debtor

Chapter One: Planning the Event

1. THE GUEST LIST

Martha Stewart says, "When you meet someone interesting at a party it is a natural reaction to think of all the other people who would like to meet him too. Sometimes I do this years in advance—putting people together in my mind." And I say to her, "Have a licensed professional sit you down and tell you all about lithium." *I* begin by inviting only those people I am so sure like me that virtually nothing I could say or do would sway their opinion. If this total does not get you beyond the fingers of one hand, add a select number of others who you know suffer from weight problems and/or eating disorders. These are people from whom heavy calorie consumption is always a problem so if you screw up the food, it won't matter. If it does happen, your guests will be secretly relieved.

2. THE MENU

Checking back in with Martha Stewart, we learn that "a dramatic spicy taste is an inappropriate way to begin dinner." Therefore, it only makes good sense to begin by offering each and every arriving guest an enormous peppery bean burrito.

"Cocktails that last much longer than an hour jeopardize the shape and momentum of the evening," Martha cautions. Since these are the very things that are most terrifying, figure on a two-hour cocktail period minimum. Now you've got everyone right where you want them: feeling fat and sleepy with a limited desire or ability to eat anything.

3. THE THEME

Martha Stewart says, "Your own dishes, possessions, and personality will determine the style and tone of the occasion." That is why I like to use as my theme "the breakup of the Soviet Union," my table settings and decorations reflecting with amazing accuracy the chaos, poverty, and desperation of a culture in the throes of disintegration.

Chapter Two: Day-of-the-Party Preparations

1. As soon as you awake, begin your futile attempt to remove the vast quantities of pet hair that have settled over everything in your house like a gentle dusting of snow on a wintry morning. Pick up as many of the saliva-coated pet toys as you can find and hide them somewhere. Anywhere. Especially the squeaking vinyl turkey leg with a face.

2. Martha Stewart thoughtfully reminds us to "Remember to empty a coat closet" to accommodate the outerwear of your guests.

   So, take all the stuff you have in there and move it to the . . . no, the garage is full. So is the bedroom closet. And the hall closet. Which is why I recommend that you just put everything *back* into the coat closet and lower the heat in the house so that your guests will not be inclined to take off their coats or sweaters.

3. Begin to anesthetize yourself. It may be politically incorrect in this day and age, but as much as you might like to, you *aren't* going to be driving anywhere. So isn't it worth it just this once to provide yourself with an impenetrable smoke screen between your problems and anxieties and your own ability to perceive them?

4. Don't forget that "music can establish and sustain an easy mood." I prefer a simple loop tape of AC/DC singing "Highway to Hell." But select your own favorites, depending on your theme.

5. Clean the pet hair off everything *again,* making sure to notice that there is just as much this time as there was before you spent all those previous hours removing it. But this time, if you are sufficiently sedated, you may enjoy taking all the saliva-coated pet toys and assembling them into a colorful centerpiece, surrounded by fresh flowers and grandmother's old silver. Place the squeaking vinyl turkey leg with a face proudly in the front. Or go directly to

PLAN B

Turn out all the lights in your house and greet arriving guests in your bathrobe and pajamas. Wearing an expression of sympathetic, quizzical bemusement, say to them. "Geez—this is kind of embarrassing. The party was *last* night. But hey—come on in. Can I get you a cup of tea?" They will probably stay only a few minutes—just long enough to get angry about already getting pet hair all over some cherished item of clothing. But because the error will seem to be *theirs,* your social obligations will be paid in full!!

Showering with
Your Dog

I don't allow just anyone with mud on his tongue to fall asleep on me. (Well, not anymore. Not since the sixties.) After several years of expensive therapy I've learned I have the right to require more from a relationship with a man. But, I must confess, it is the mark of how completely in love I am with my dog, Stan, that I almost always find this kind of behavior endearing in him.

Stan's status in my household has been steadily on the rise ever since that black day in September when the indoor dog population of my home was reduced by 50 percent. That was when half of my two head of dog went off to the giant overturned garbage can in the sky. At first I was concerned that the remaining member of the team would be lonely, troubled, maybe racked with guilt, the way Timothy Hutton's surviving-brother character was in *Ordinary People*. Then I began to observe that Stan was actually kind of glad Bob was gone.

I shouldn't have been too surprised. After all, on frighteningly frequent occasions over the years, Stan had, in a pretty straightforward fashion, tried to kill Bob. I always wrote off these murder attempts as poor impulse control rather than genuine malice-aforethought, homicidal-type acts. But now that it's completely apparent how much he enjoys the perks that come with being a solo dog act, I'm not so sure, especially after witnessing him nearly kill the puppy I briefly tried to add to our strange little family. And the fact is, he really *does* get perks now. For instance, I used to find it much easier to get into my car dogless when there were *two* dogs standing at the front door making those "We'd rather be dead than be left here" faces. I would think to myself, *Ah, screw it. They'll be fine. They'll entertain each other.* Then I'd leave the house with a clear conscience, imagining some kind of secret doggy confabs that came alive only in my absence—maybe intense, animated discussions of heartworm or something.

But when Stan stands *alone* at the front door making that "How can you do this to me?" face, I almost never drive off dog-free. My anthropomorphic fantasies rage much more violently out of control now that there's just one dog. Even at the expense of the reasonable maintenance of my car, which at this point is evenly coated with dog hair, even under the hood and inside all of the spark plugs.

On the plus side, riding around with Stan can be fun. It's certainly much less stressful than riding around with the average man. For example, he always lets me pick the radio station, and he greets my every choice of destination with boundless enthusiasm. And there are those special times when he leans over to nuzzle me with his snout—which I always take to be an incredibly moving tribute to the amazing bond that our species are able to share . . . until I remember, too late, that most of the times he does this he is simply looking for a cozy place to throw up. The most memorable instance of this was the time I was having the house fumigated for fleas and had been instructed not to go back inside for four hours. And so I was left trying to figure out an afternoon of activities appropriate for a woman covered with dog vomit.

I guess the point I'm getting to is that I'm completely off the deep end as a dog parent now that there is just the one dog, because in a lot of ways he seems like more of a roommate. And as a roommate, I have to say he's doing a nice job. Anything I prepare for dinner seems perfect to him. From a handful of popcorn to fettucine Alfredo to small, hard bits of gristle in a plate of warm beer (a personal specialty), he has never failed to exhibit anything less than exuberant delight in my menu planning. No man was ever this easy to please, that's for sure.

Okay, yes, there is a certain amount of unsavory cleaning to do out in the backyard, but it's actually minor compared to what's required after a man has blasted through a house like a raging tornado. And, yes, he does leave a lot of hair and stuff on the bed, but he also never hogs the remote control and forces me to watch hours of TV shows in five-second increments.

Unfortunately, there's a complication. Since I have conferred on Stan the status of roommate it has become increasingly difficult to compel him to undergo traditional dog humiliations. Like bathing. I used to tie the boy up in the yard and hose him down (the way you might, say, your parents) but that no longer seems fair. No basic pet-care book deals with this type of readjustment. And since it is my goal here to fill the holes that others never knew existed, I would like to help bring pet care into the nineties, advising those for whom a pet is a significant other. Or if not, certainly an insignificant one. My first topic: showering with your dog.

Let's face it. Even the most beloved dog can be very stinky at times. And where pet hygiene is concerned, the enlightened pet guardian (and, of course, by that I mean me) has no choice but to share the indoor facilities with the animal.

Step 1:
Choosing the Proper Wardrobe

When showering with your dog, it *is* advisable to wear swimwear. I don't know whether the dog would know if you were naked, but *you* would know.

Step 2:
Getting the Dog into the Shower

Nothing can really proceed until this is accomplished. Often the dog will exhibit a little initial reluctance . . . perhaps because he has watched too many horror movies on TV in which showers are presented in an unfortunate light. Many dogs have never given any thought to the concept of "fiction" and so do not know that most showers are not just another death trap. Rather than confront the animal with a lot of mind-blowing philosophical concepts, I recommend one of two less complicated strategies that work for me. The first is what I call the old "ball in the shower" approach, in which you, the parent or guardian, relocate to the inside of the shower with some favorite sports equipment, making it appear that you have selected the location *not* because of its showering capabilities but simply because it is the best damn place for miles around to hit fungoes. If, after fifteen or twenty minutes of enthusiastic solo sports maneuvers, you have not managed to interest the animal in joining you, I suggest you switch to the immediately effective "chicken skin around the drain" approach. It's a well-documented fact that only a minute amount of chicken skin can accumulate in the lower third of any area of the world before it will be joined by a dog.

Once this has happened, simply close the shower door behind him, or pull the curtain. (For the more squeamish among you who worry about the mess in the shower, you can count on the dog to clean it all up. If he should happen to miss a little, and some chicken skin remains, don't worry. It will simply be taken by any future showerers as a remarkable indication of how seriously you scrub yourself when you wash.)

Step 3:
Moistening and
Soaping the Animal

This may be trickier than it appears, because the animal tends to move to the parts of the shower where there is no water. And so it becomes your perpetual task to keep moving the water to the parts of the shower where there is a dog. During this phase, apply shampoo and try not to take personally the animal's expression, which indicates a hatred and loathing so extreme that he is trying to figure out how he can reconnect with his long-buried primitive instincts to kill and eat a human being. It may be useful to let the dog know that showering is not a punishment but something *you* actually find pleasurable and relaxing. If this does not help, now is an excellent time to explain to the animal that the legal system is built primarily around the rights of humans, and, if you want to, you can take him back to the pound where you got him and then his life won't be worth a plugged nickel.

Step 4:
Rinsing

You are now dealing with increasing desperation on the part of the dog, who may be getting ready to make a break for it. This is why nature gave the dog a tail, to help you as you try to restrain him before he runs through the house all matted and soapy and gets big hair-encrusted stains all over your cherished possessions.

Step 5:
Toweling the Dog

This process is designed to help you avoid the splattered, soaking mess that results when the dog shakes himself off. No matter how diligently you perform toweling, it is futile. When you're through, the dog will disperse the same astonishing amounts of water and hair as if he had never been toweled at all.

Now you may release the animal, perhaps deluding yourself that he is thrilled at his cleaner condition. You should return immediately to the shower and shovel out the three to five pounds of hair you will find lodged in your drain. This brings me to the final but most important step.

Step 6:
Remove Any Bottles of Flea and Tick Shampoo

Take it from someone who has lived through every unfortu-nate scenario that can result from simply leaving the bottle around. This needs to be memorized and remembered. . . . I know I have helped you.

Sexual Secrets
and Other
Self-improvements

Here's something that New York and Los Angeles have in common that hardly ever makes the comparison charts: Both have big piles of free extension-school course schedules sitting out on streets and in stores everywhere. I have been grabbing them for years now, simply for the pleasure of taking them home and saying in animated tones to myself, *"Who attends these things?"*

For example: "Writing Erotica: Sizzle Sells." Who the hell shows up at that one? And what do they even *mean* by teaching a course called "Charisma: How to Achieve That Special Magic"? So I thought I'd find out. I turned down "Learn About Your Season Through Color" and "Start Your Own Cooking Business . . . Now!" in favor of a couple that looked even more intriguing. As luck would have it, I turned up at part two of each course.

1. "Sexual Secrets of the Orient"

As I walk up a flight of stairs in the lobby of a large hotel near the Los Angeles International Airport, I can't help viewing everyone else headed up the stairs with suspicion. Are they here for the sexual secrets, too, and if so, why? Are they dangerous? Which is why, when I meet the instructor (in a meeting room full of rows of gold oval-backed hotel chairs), I am surprised. She is a short, stocky woman with no-nonsense graying hair and large earrings. She speaks with the deliberate manner of a grade school teacher, and she insists on giving me a name tag. "I don't want you to be just a no one," she tells me, not realizing that I am not the type to want a high-profile image at a class called "Sexual Secrets of the Orient."

Slowly the other class members are filtering in . . . and they are a pleasant-looking group of mostly white adults between the ages of twenty-five and forty-five—about half men and half women. There's a guy in a loud sport coat who looks like Dabney Coleman, two couples who look like Esalen Institute graduates, four cute guys in their twenties who seem to have come by themselves, and the regulation number of perky single women.

The instructor, whose name is Ginny Dingman and who is an R.N. with some degrees in human sexuality, begins to grill the assembled group. "Did you all write a sexual fantasy this week? Yes? No? *Please* remember to do that *this* week because it really gets the sexual energies flowing. What about drawing a picture of yourselves? Did you all look at yourselves in the mirror like you were supposed to?" She suggests to us that the women in the class might like to develop a nickname for their sexual organs. "The guys sometimes have names for their dick or their peter," she tells us, "so you can have a name, too. Like maybe Matilda. Or Melissa." She pushes her glasses up into her hair and walks up and down the aisle. "How many of you played with yourself this week? I want you to make a contract with yourself that you're going to play with yourself two to three times a week. Come on, guys! You laid cold hard cash down!" As she distributes our first handout I am thinking to myself that these secrets of the Orient are a lot more accessible than I had figured. Now we read about the pubococcygeal muscle, which, she tells us, is used to start and stop the flow of urine. "I'll call it the Kegel muscle, and I want you to start becoming a Kegel muscle exerciser on the freeway with me. I am working my Kegel muscle right now, as I talk to you. And when I get stuck in freeway traffic I just sit there going Kegel, Kegel, Kegel, Kegel, Kegel."

As cute as she is (and she is cute), she does have a compulsion to tell the class more personal information than I have ever really wanted to know about one of my teachers. We learn that she is fifty-seven and has a fifty-nine-year-old husband who has no erectile problems, that she was a bed wetter until she was sixteen and never had an orgasm until she was forty-eight, that it takes her a long time to lubricate, that she was once in a car wreck that gave her horrible intestinal problems and constipation for a time, and that she and her husband did drawings of their sexual organs that now hang proudly in the bathroom of their home. The class is a one-woman tour de force for Ginny, who, at other points during the evening, massages one guy's back, one woman's leg, and another woman's butt, walks around the room touching everyone with a vibrator, shows us how to bounce testicles in our hands, demonstrates a palms-on-the-nipples massage technique on her own ample breasts, and previews for us a wealth of unusual poems and reading materials, including but not limited to the *Cunt Coloring Book.*

Things do take a turn for the slightly more Oriental as we move on to the semi-exotic Ben Wa balls. "When I first started wearing these I had had four babies and three abdominal surgeries," Ginny says, holding a set up, "and I had no muscle tone in there. And they'd fall right out. I was the goose that laid the golden eggs." Ben Wa balls, she tells us, were developed by Oriental women to strengthen the Kegel muscle. "So what happens is they roll around and go doodledy-doodledy-doo." "What do they feel like?" a woman in the class wants to know. "Thank you very much for asking that," says Ginny, who explains that during intercourse men find them pleasurable but women report it doesn't feel that great. "Is there any way they can be pushed in so you can't get them out?" asks another woman. "Oh gosh, you ask wonderful questions!" says Ginny, who counsels us that if they do get lost, "just take a bath. Wash the dishes. Don't worry. They'll come out."

During the break I talk to a thin, waiflike blond woman who says she prefers being called Ocean (although her name tag reads AGNES). She tells me she is a private tutor in reading improvement, vocabulary building, and intellectual enrichment who is taking the class to aid in her quest to become a "four-star A-double-plus lover," because she believes that "being a disciple of Aphrodite is one of the best uses of your time while you're here on Earth."

The cute guy with the beard who is sitting in front of me turns out to be a business-machine repairman who came here from Russia seven years ago. He doesn't think they had any similar classes in the Soviet Union, but he does feel he picked up some useful tips here tonight. He has previously enrolled in windsurfing and hiking classes.

As it turns out, there are many repeat offenders among course graduates. The blond woman in front (who appears to be with her girlfriend) says she has also taken "Letting Go and Moving On" and "Direct Mail: The Marketing Phenomenon of the Decade."

"Thanks a lot, guys. We did it!" are Ginny's parting words to us, at about 10 P.M. And off into the night walk twenty-five strangers, all bearing sexual secrets.

2. "Looking for Someone: A Career as a Private Detective"

The description in the book said, "Learn surveillance, interview, interrogation and undercover techniques."

The class is being held at the Nick Harris Detective Academy, which turns out to be a small brick building in the San Fernando Valley. There, inside a regulation-style classroom, a small wiry-haired man named Milo Speriglio is standing at a podium. Despite the fact that there are only fourteen people attending tonight, he is addressing the class with a microphone. A plaque attached to the front of the podium says NICK HARRIS DETECTIVE AGENCY. SINCE 1911. Against the back wall of the classroom is a giant banner that reads NICK HARRIS DETECTIVE AGENCY. SINCE 1907. I am a couple of minutes late arriving so I sneak to an empty desk; on it is an "information kit," the front page of which says NICK HARRIS DETECTIVES. FOUNDED IN 1906. But never mind. Milo correctly identifies me as the woman who is coming from a magazine. "What magazine are you with?" he asks me. *"New York Woman,"* I answer. "Oh," he says, "I didn't know it was a woman's magazine. Is it M-r-s or M-s or M-i-s-s? I was once interviewed by Gloria Steinberg." "No," I tell him, "it's called *New York Woman* magazine." "Does it have anything to do with *Playboy* or *Playgirl*?" he asks me. I can see a pack of Kool cigarettes through the pocket of his translucent yellow shirt. On each of his wrists is a crushed-gold wristband: one watch, one bracelet. He is also wearing several rings. Now Milo holds up a pen. "Anyone know what this is?" he asks. No one is dumb enough to say "A pen." Someone says, "A transmitter?" "It has been determined that Marilyn Monroe was murdered," Milo answers, "and using my magic pen—I just touch the top of it—" He does so and activates an audiotape of some interviews he conducted during his apparently endless investigation of this case. For the next fifteen or twenty minutes we listen to a man he calls his "deep throat" and another guy who says one of his ambulances drove Monroe's body. He gives more obscure information than I ever wanted about this particular incident. "Was she starting to turn blue?" Milo asks the ambulance guy. "Well, the patient would inevitably turn blue, yes" is part of what I hear before I begin to tune it all out. A blond woman in the next row is picking hairs off her giant shoulder pads. The class is predominantly female: eleven women in summerwear and three men who look considerably grungier. When the tape is over, Milo asks for questions and someone asks for more information about "pretext," a concept that was apparently introduced last week, at the first part of this course. Milo says he *might* give additional examples were it not for the presence of a certain magazine reporter.

Milo now entertains us with anecdotes regarding his own wacky escapades . . . like the time he made an illegal U-turn on Sunset Boulevard: "I'm being chased and so I take out my credentials . . . which look very close to that of another investigative bureau—I forgot the name of it but the initials are FBI . . ."

"Any more questions?" A thirtyish man in a Mickey Mouse T-shirt shoots up his hand. During an upcoming break I learn that his name is Jim and that he is a plumber from Pomona. Jim thinks that being a private detective might be a more interesting job, "for a while anyway." (No newcomer to the world of extension programs, Jim last attended a course in "Makeup and Skin Care," where he learned to "drink lots of water and use certain creams and stuff like that.") Now he wants to know if some detectives use multiple identities. "Yes," says Milo, "when they're using subterfuge or pretext. They won't come out and say, 'I'm John Smith.' They might say, 'I'm *Jack* Smith' or something like that."

As the class goes on, Jim has a great many questions to ask. He wants to know if hypnosis can help you beat a lie detector. He wants to know if you can file your fingerprints off or whether the application of glue will cause them to disappear. He wants to know whether galoshes will eliminate footprints. I begin to wonder, *Why exactly does he want to know?*

Now Fawn wants to know if Milo has worked on "cases of international proportions." She is wearing a ponytail pulled to one side of her head. Just this week she got dumped from her job in sales, and, she tells me, she has enrolled as a full-time student here. "Yes," says Milo. "Can you give some examples?" she asks. "No," he says, eliciting light laughter. I talk to the hennaed woman with braces and checkerboard socks who is seated behind me. She is Candy, a woman who has taught grade school for seventeen years, but thinks that someday she might like to have another career. Now she feels she wouldn't really want to be a private detective because she doesn't really like the idea of using pretense in dealing with people.

Before the class ends Milo shows us how to write on money with a crayon that can only be seen in ultraviolet light, and demonstrates equipment that makes a beep when it gets near hidden bugs or wiretaps. I realize I have been regularly checking my watch to see how late it is getting, pretty much the way I used to do when I was in high school. On my way out I chat with a stocky fiftyish woman named Judy Johnston, who tells me she just retired from her job as an accounts-payable clerk. Judy looks as unlikely a candidate for a career as a private detective as any living creature has a right to. But she tells me she has always been interested in the field. And so she was disappointed. "I felt we didn't really learn a whole lot. I feel like I paid forty dollars for very little. But I'm interested in taking the investigator course," she says as she unlocks her car.

What I Have Learned from My Studies

1. FBI agents bend their car antennae so they will recognize each other.
2. Woman-on-top and rear-entry-knees-to-chest are the best positions for getting hit in the G-spot.
3. It's easiest to take criminal fingerprints off a dead body.
4. Four women that Ginny Dingman knows set off airport

metal detectors by trying to go through wearing Ben
Wa balls.

5. The most dangerous form of private-eye work is process
serving.

6. There is an Oriental sexual practice in which you take a
silk string with knots in it and insert it up your lover's
rectum. At the moment of orgasm you slowly pull it out.
The key word here is "slowly," for you can pull out a person's intestinal tract, which, for people like me, is really a
giant turnoff. In fact, I'm not sure that some of these darn
sexual secrets weren't better off when they were secrets.

Something Extremely Important

Today our friend Paul came to the house in a nearly dissociative state of panic. Suddenly and without warning, it appeared that his marriage was unraveling.

He sat down on the big red couch in the living room, I offered him a vodka, and he cautiously began to detail his anguish.

"Up until yesterday, if you had asked me if my marriage was a happy one, I would have said yes," he said, choking back tears, his voice quivering with emotion, "and then last night, out of the blue, my wife comes in and tells me she wants a divorce."

As Paul spoke, our dog Puppyboy, a skinny brown-and-black Tijuana Shepherd, approached with his mouth full of a large, black, completely deflated soccer ball. He placed the flat wet piece of rubber gently on Paul's knee, where it balanced like a rock at Stonehenge. Then he sat down right in front of Paul to wait for the games to begin. To Puppyboy, a ball is still a ball whether or not it is currently filled with air, and any opportunity is as good as any other to begin a game of "Toss the Deflated Soccer Ball Across the Room."

Paul was too upset to notice. "She told me she wants to start seeing other men," he said, tears welling up in his eyes, "and that's not even the worst of it. Today I found out from friends that they have already seen her around town with another guy. They didn't want to say anything until now."

He began to cry. It was heartrending. Except to Puppyboy, who saw it as a cue to apply a little additional pressure. So he picked up the deflated piece of rubber off the edge of Paul's knee and moved it to a new spot, a little farther up Paul's leg, thereby putting it just a teensy bit closer to Paul's hands, for his convenience. Just in case Paul hadn't noticed it all the way down there on his knee. And, having rectified the problem, Puppyboy sat back down in front of Paul and resumed the ceaseless staring that he felt confident would now cause the game to start.

But Paul had the bad manners to be completely preoccupied by his own tragedy.

"I have no idea what I am going to do," he said, as Puppyboy moved in a little closer and began staring a little harder, his eyes going intently from the flat black rubber thing that was balancing on Paul's thigh, to Paul's face, and then back to the flat black rubber thing, as if to help Paul out in case he was having trouble locating it.

"It's been just emotionally devastating," Paul continued. "Everything I've worked for has fallen apart. And what happens to me now? Am I going to lose everything? My house? My cars? My life savings?" He broke down and began to sob: the only time I have ever seen this incredibly stoic man cry.

Which was a signal to Puppyboy that the game was finally about to get going, so he picked up the deflated soccer ball off Paul's thigh and moved it to the most conveniently located spot of all, the very center of Paul's lap. Then he sat back down in front of Paul and resumed his intense staring, his face as bright with expectation as a preschooler's on Christmas morning.

The more gruesome Paul's story became, the more over-whelming his pain, the more convinced Puppyboy was that game time was near. He *knew* that by moving that flat wet piece of rubber that used to be a ball to slightly different places on Paul's legs, and then staring with what amounted to X-ray vision, he had a winning combination that was ultimately irresistible.

So he kept doing this for the whole two hours that Paul was at our house discussing his recent catastrophe, despite the fact that Paul never acknowledged him at all.

Later that night, after Paul had gone home to pick up the pieces of his shattered existence, I began to wonder what Pup-pyboy was thinking during this piece of behavior, which was akin to trying to start a game of catch with a man whose entire body was trapped under a fifty-ton boulder. So I asked him.

Puppyboy Speaks

Hello, new seated person. I am Puppyboy and I can see that you are very upset for some reason. But I have something on my mind.

It is an idea so big that I can hardly hold my head up from the enormous weight of it. It is *more* than an idea. It is an *ur-gent message*. I am going out on a limb here to tell you that it is *the most important thing I have ever had to say.* And it is this: *I have placed a thing on you that you must throw.*

If you look down now, you will see it. It is the large flat thing that is balancing on your knee. It is stretchy and chewy and damp: everything a large flat thing should be. Please listen to me when I tell you *that this is an opportunity you cannot pass up.*

The reason I feel I must tell you *that I have placed this large flat thing on the edge of your knee*—by the way, you *have noticed* that your knee has a big flat wet thing balancing on it, haven't you? Or are you so busy sobbing and weeping and talking about *yourself* that you are having trouble seeing it?

Here's a hint: I am staring at it right now. So if you can imagine a laser beam coming from my eyes and then follow it down to the spot on your leg where it is focused, it will lead you right to it. . . .

There.

Now, either you see it or you need to get your eyes tested. The only other possible explanation for your puzzling lack of interest is that you are purposely ignoring me. And why would you do that? *That* doesn't make any sense. Especially since you are really hurting yourself more than you are hurting me. Because, let's face it, you're the one who is passing up a great opportunity. And by "a great opportunity" I am referring to the chance to have the kind of fun that everyone dreams of having. *I speak of the chance to throw a big flat stretchy wet thing. Think about it for a second.*

It is a thing that can be chewed but does not really need to be swallowed.

It is at once like dinner and nothing like dinner at all.

It is tough and meatlike and moist like a dead thing, but, here's the kicker: It's *all of the fun* of a dead thing and none of the attendant trouble. It stinks like a dead thing, and you can roll on it, or take it with you to bed like a dead thing.

It can be stretched and laid upon and pulled apart like a dead thing. But it *can also be flung repeatedly, without coming*

apart in a million pieces and losing all its guts like a dead thing.
Can you believe your good luck? AND guess where it is right
now? *It is right in your lap.* I can't believe you would be foolish
enough to pass up this chance.

I don't want to be preachy, but in life there are certain moments that may never come again. This, I believe, is one of
those moments for you. Throw it now or live a life of regret.

I mean, I can't *stop you* if you'd rather just listen to yourself
talk. Wife wife wife, she did this, she did that, great.

FOR CHRISSAKES LISTEN TO ME, *YOU WHINY,
HENPECKED MOTHERFUCKER. Just look into my eyes, and
play along! Pick up the big flat wet thing.*

Pick up the big flat wet thing.

*Pick up the big flat wet thing. PICK IT UP. PICK IT UP.
PICK UP THE BIG FLAT WET THING!*

*CAN YOU HEAR ME OKAY? PICK UP THE BIG FLAT
WET THING.*

*Are you even listening? You know, maybe if you had LIS-
TENED A LITTLE BETTER DURING YOUR MARRIAGE
your wife wouldn't want a divorce. DID you ever think of that?
IT WOULDN'T SURPRISE ME IF YOU NEVER THREW
THE THINGS THAT SHE BROUGHT YOU EITHER!*

Okay. I admit that was hitting below the belt.

So that was not the only chance you will get. I am going to
give you another chance right away, as you will see, if you will
but gaze legward.

I have *again* placed the big flat wet thing on your thigh and
now you will find it is even more conveniently located than
before.

And listen, pal, if I were you, I wouldn't pass up an incredible opportunity like this again.

An Insider's Guide
to the
American Woman

The first item in my collection of the greatest irritants of the early nineties is the June 1990 issue of *Esquire* featuring "The Secret Life of the American Wife." On the cover is a partially clothed woman, anatomically labeled with such questions as "HER LIPS: Can you trust what they say?" and "HER BRA: What *really* keeps it up?"

I'm not surprised to learn that men are still mystified by women. Certainly women are still utterly baffled by men. But what I found so infuriating this time around was the type of thing the (presumably college-educated) editors and writers were pretending to find so gosh-darned unfathomable. And their approach! So *retro,* so fifties, so "Honey, now dry those tears and how about we take you downtown and buy you something sparkly?"

The lead article ("Your Wife: An Owner's Manual") offered pseudoscientific dissections of such feminine mysteries as "HER HANDBAG: Its capacity and contents" and "HER PLUMB-ING: General diagnostics." If this is how far men have come in their knowledge of women—to wide-eyed wonderment at the contents of her purse and dumbfounded speechlessness at the thought of "female plumbing"—well, I personally think now is as good a time as any to throw in the towel.

My suggestion to men is, *Stop trying* to comprehend that which is clearly too complicated for you. Let me kindly state that it no longer really matters whether or not you understand. I just don't think you should worry your pretty little heads about it for another moment. Instead, simply *memorize* the following information and blindly incorporate it into your thinking, much as one might deal with an elusive scientific concept, such as $E = mc^2$.

Merrill's Fun Facts to Know and Tell About Women

1. Women and the English Language. To a woman, the words "I had a great time. I'll call you" translate roughly to mean, "He said he had a great time. He'll call me." So, if you *say* those words, expect to *make* a call to the woman to whom you have said them. If this does not fit into your plans, *do not say those words.* (I know this is confusing. Just memorize it and do it. There's nothing more to discuss.)

Women have other quirky language-oriented notions. For instance, to a woman the words "I love you" represent a heartfelt expression of the intensely fond feelings you have for her. At least, this kind of thing will be what the woman has in mind when *she* utters the words, and so she will not be pleased if your response is "Thank you" or "I know."

There is an interesting truth behind some of this that may

be hard to grasp: Women *like* to talk about personal things. In fact, they actually *listen* when a man does just that. Why? Well, because women believe that a conversation can go beyond a simple exchange of sports scores! Yes! They do! In fact, women who meet for the first time on a checkout line will often have more intimate conversations with each other than they have had with men to whom they have been married for two or three decades. They do this voluntarily! Why? Because they find it *enjoyable*!

Now that you understand this, realize that the answer to "Hi, honey. What did you do today?" is *not* "I don't know. Nothing."

2. Women and Food. Most women are on a diet, thinking about going on a diet, or wondering if they should think about going on a diet. In a free-market economy, a majority of women will order a salad on a majority of dining-out occasions. If a man wishes a woman to change her eating habits and make them more like his own, he need only repackage the food he would like to see eaten as a salad. For example, most women would feel okay about sitting down to a hot-fudge-sundae salad or a pizza salad.

It is not necessary to inquire whether a woman would like something for dessert. The answer is, *yes,* she *would* like something for dessert, but she would like *you* to order it so she can pick at it with her fork. She does not want you to call attention to this by saying, "If you wanted a dessert, why didn't you order one?" You must understand, she *has* the dessert she wants. The dessert she wants is contained *within* yours!

Bear in mind also that she wants you to keep pace with her and prefers you to eat at least half of your dessert because she does *not* want the responsibility of having eaten most of it.

3. Their Entertainment Needs. Unlike men, most women are not endlessly in search of opportunities to watch things crash and blow up. Women tend to prefer movies teeming with human intrigue and personal foible to movies where someone breaks through a plate glass window with a car, or breaks a plate glass window with his fist, or breaks someone's head with his fist in a car, or breaks someone's fist with a plate glass window. We're just wacky that way.

4. Women's Ablutions (and why they take so long). The amount of time a woman takes to prepare for a date with a man is in direct proportion to the amount of time she has spent observing that man staring saucer-eyed at other women who have put in at least the aforementioned amount of preparation time on their date. If a man would like to see one decrease, so too must the other.

5. Their Plumbing. How much should you know? Women are the ones who do not have a penis and did not even have to undergo painful penis-removal surgery to accomplish this. As a result, they will require more frequent stops on a long car trip.

Once a month women find themselves strangely depressed and taking a long hard look at where they've made a wrong turn in life. They will ruminate over such dilemmas as "Perhaps the reason I'm depressed is that I really need to find a better job, but I guess I'm afraid to change because I have such low self-esteem, which comes from my childhood when my mother always used to tell me blah blah blah blah blah." Then they realize they have just gotten their period, which snuck up on them in the form of a mood change. So if you get involved with a woman, don't be surprised when you find it sneaking up on you as well.

There are very simple ways to give a woman an orgasm.

These involve specific manipulations of "the plumbing." If you suspect that you don't know what you're doing but think you are bluffing effectively and/or you notice that it is taking more than a half hour, please be advised that you're fooling *no one*. It's just that most women are too polite and too concerned about the frailties of the male ego to say anything. So ask the owner of "the plumbing" to provide you with some helpful tips!!! And save everyone involved a couple of long, painful hours!!! And by the way . . . if you *do* suspect that you don't know what you're doing, for God's sake, don't do it *harder*.

6. Women and Love. I have heard men say that they don't mind the idea of breast implants in a woman because, after all, big breasts are big breasts. (Actually what I have heard men say is slightly coarser.) On the other hand, I have never met a woman who would rather be with a man in a toupee than a bald man.

This ability to accept and embrace the less-than-ideal, this generosity of spirit, has a downside—the tendency to be attracted to psychos. We know better, we're not proud of this, and we have spent decades learning that we would *really* rather be with nice men. But any man who has a problem attracting women because they think he is too nice would do well to augment his usual behavior with anguished exhalations of barely controlled rage.

In case you haven't noticed, women take sex just a tad more personally than do guys. For a woman, the only working definition of a one-night stand is a night spent with a guy who turned out to be a total weenie. The degree of any date's success can be easily determined by the degree of obsession it causes in the woman. If you would like to test this, introduce yourself to some of her good friends. If they aren't already sick of hearing your name, *the date didn't go that well*.

Once women are in love, they can be easily manipulated because they're so overwhelmed with feelings of insecurity. Many will happily take responsibility for everything that goes wrong, as in: "If he isn't happy it's my fault" and "If I'm not happy it's my fault."

Now that you know this, be a good guy and don't take unfair advantage. *Own up to stuff you know is your fault.* You might as well, anyway, because there is still another female phenomenon that ensures you'll be living on borrowed time if you don't.

7. Women and Therapy. Women are naturally attracted to therapy. Yes, it's true! If they don't get expensive one-on-one counseling, they will read self-help books and magazine articles or listen to radio and TV shows that discuss these issues or talk to and get advice from their friends who have done some or all of the above. Women do this because therapy actually involves so many of the things they enjoy: personal idiosyncrasy, a chance to talk dramatically about themselves, and a good starting point for future conversations with friends or anyone they might meet in the checkout line.

8. Their Purses, Their Bras. A woman learns at a young age that she will be expected to carry the equivalent of a suitcase everywhere she goes for the rest of her life. And so she plans accordingly, secure in the knowledge that she will permanently have at her disposal anything, under a certain size, she might need in an emergency. This means that no matter what unexpected event or disaster she encounters, a woman will always have enough makeup to look really cute.

As far as the bra goes . . . give me a break, okay? *Give me a fucking break.*

A Dog Is a Dog
Is a Dog

For months now I have been living in dog adoption hell. I sure hope I'm not going to be a permanent resident.

As anyone who has ever read more than two pieces of my work has probably noticed, I have kind of a dog fixation. Which I guess made it all the worse this past Thanksgiving when I lost my remaining dog. Well, I didn't really *lose* him. I *know* where he is. He's dead of a toxic overdose of ham.

Yes, you read correctly. My boy was killed by a house sitter who stupidly left about half a HoneyBaked Ham in dog-stealing proximity. Once you know that toxic levels of fat in a prepared ham can destroy the pancreas, liver, and kidneys of a seventy-five-pound dog, that ad featuring a smiling, tuxedoed O. J. Simpson holding up a giant silver serving tray of the stuff suddenly looks like a still from *A Nightmare on Elm Street.*

I guess holiday gluttony was one weakness that both my dogs had in common. A few years back, my older dog, Bob, stole and consumed a ten-pound frozen turkey. Luckily for him, turkey has a very low fat content, and the worst side effect he suffered was the short-term embarrassment of looking briefly like a medium-size sofa bed.

Still, I was not at all prepared for Stan's death. He was in good health when I went away for Thanksgiving. And dead when I returned. It was the first time I had ever spent a minute in my house without him.

My life with Stan began when I realized that Bob didn't bark when people came into my yard. Only squirrels. I took some comfort in the fact that I was covered if a psycho dressed in a squirrel suit broke into my house, but I decided to bring in a backup line of defense. So I went to the pound and, in about fifteen seconds, plucked Stan off death row. He was the shyest, saddest-looking dog in a giant cage full of future dead guys. He also had a pair of ears on him that could have carried him airborne.

I think I selected him so quickly because his passive-aggressive approach broadcast the phrase "Rescue Me" louder than the energetic, friendlier efforts of all his cell mates. I had not yet realized that I was using the same method to select dogs that I was using to select men—with some of the same problematic results. Eventually Stan turned out to have un-controllable homicidal urges toward others of his species. How often has a date of mine been ruined by much the same thing?

Stan followed me everywhere, seeming to be operating with the mentality of someone who had either been aban-doned or gotten badly lost and who was *not* going to make that mistake again. When I got into my pool to swim laps, he jumped in after me. From that point on he *never* let me out of his sight if he could help it. Day or night, even when I went into the bathroom, I could always count on the fact that Stan would be standing somewhere nearby, *staring* at me as though he felt something *good* was going to happen. This was his trademark. It always made me feel guilty because in most cases I knew damn well that nothing particularly good had been planned.

And so I had to live with the constant knowledge that I was continually letting him down. If I reached for a Kleenex, Stan would jump to his feet, certain that this was the first move in a potentially thrilling chain of events. He had an abiding belief that every action in this world might eventually lead to food or ball. In fact, he made this so clear to me that a fair percentage of the time I did try to follow up whatever I was doing with a little food or ball. Happily, he died without ever having learned the cruel truth that taking out the garbage or opening up the sock drawer does not *necessarily* signal any dog activity.

To his credit, Stan was an excellent ballplayer. Whereas Bob used to play "Catch the Ball and Eat It," Stan preferred "Double Dog Ball," in which two balls are put into play at all times, the one in the mouth being released at the same time that the one in the hand hits the air. This game could go on indefinitely—in fact, the more indefinitely the better. And because he was so enthusiastic in his playing, I generally chose to overlook the fact that he almost always took a dump on the dog ball field, during the third inning, with the ball still in his mouth. Anyone who has ever played this game will tell you that ordinarily this is an automatic out.

Also, thanks to Stan, I developed a certain confidence about my sloppy eating habits, secure in the knowledge that any food accidentally dropped onto the lower half of the room would instantaneously become his property. And because I was expected to give him a substantial portion of everything I was eating, I never really had to worry about consuming too many calories. Of course this was often just one more way in which I was a source of disappointment to him, since all he'd wind up with was a portion of some dumb salad. He'd eat it, but he wasn't happy about it. I bet the day that HoneyBaked Ham turned up at my house must have seemed to him like some kind of answered prayer.

When he died, I sobbed for a couple of days, then everyone advised me to get "out there" and find myself a new dog. On day one of my search I called a series of ads from the *Los Angeles Times* that turned out to have been placed by a variety of kind ladies who feel compelled to rescue strays and then to attempt to find people to adopt them. This sounded like some kind of scam to me until I visited the suburban residence of a fiftyish Japanese lady who had two dogs in her front yard, two dogs in her backyard, one in her garage, five in her house, and one in her station wagon. Since I had no automatic instinct about which of them to take, I decided not to rush things and left to think it over.

The next day on my way home from work I stopped by the animal shelter nearest to my home and met dozens of other dogs, all cute. All potentially mine.

Overwhelmed again, I headed home alone. In the days that followed I repeated this behavior on a daily basis. Plus I added a way to confuse myself even further—I began taking some of the candidates out to a special yard to see if we had any "chemistry." That was when I learned that, though a dog may nuzzle you through the cage, when he is released from a kennel situation, he can offer you, at best, the kind of behavior I used to get from my own dogs when they were finally released from the vet. They would rush right on past in a sort of dog tornado, ignoring me totally in a mad dash to get the hell out. As depressing as it always was to receive that treatment from a beloved family pet, to have a strange dog treat you that way is even more peculiar. Not only does no chemistry occur, it is hard not to worry that maybe this new dog hates your guts. Anyway, after these experiences I decided to go home and think about it.

Then I paid a visit to something called the Pet Adoption Fund, in the San Fernando Valley, a large kennel facility where a lot of kind ladies board about 300 different dogs and cats that they have rescued. Walking past cage after cage of candidates I felt like a member of the parole board meeting thousands of eligible prisoners. Dog after dog would scream to me:

"I'm a big, dumb guy. Take me home and I'll kiss you, then eat all your furniture."

"I'm more sedate, but I'm kind of an older guy. I don't know you and I'm not sure I like you."

"I *love* you. Here, watch me make this dog face. See? No one can resist it."

They were *all* going a million miles an hour.

That was the day it occurred to me that what I was actually looking for, in their faces, was the face of *my* dog. I was looking for that familiar stare that already knew me, already knew how to live with me and could come home and fit in and put things back the way they were. Which is why that was also the day I decided to knock off looking for a while. Because the reality is that there are *millions* of dogs who could be completely right for me. One thing you would have had to say about my two dogs was that they could easily be classified as "generic." But in the decades we spent together they each became so completely lovable and unique that each was irreplaceable. And in a way their very randomness makes the new selection process tougher. How in the world do I figure out which dog to save? I guess one day I'll just show up at one of these facilities and point and say, "That one." And then I'll have my new dog.

Ninety-eight percent of the dogs I meet are probably perfect. The whole key is that somehow *I* have to be ready.

I, Lewis

My name is Lewis, and it was initially my plan to live with Barbara Bush in the White House. But she was a no-show. So I came to live with Merrill Markoe instead. It was January 1991, and her previous dog, Stan, had died a couple months earlier from a toxic overdose of ham. None dare call it suicide.

I feel I should say at this point that I have found people pretty strange from the first, but this woman is nuts, and I mean that sincerely.

So anyway, I was about seven weeks old (which is like 150 of your years), and I go to sleep one night and the next day when I wake up I'm in solitary. I mean, I realized I was big for my age, but I'll be damned if I know what I did. One minute I'm being born. The next I'm a lifer. And I'm the youngest one in the joint. I don't know what stunt I pulled during my nap, but I think it was a doozy.

So I'm in the slammer and not much is happening. People stop by and stick their hands through the bars in my cell, and

I gnaw on their fingers with my razor-sharp teeth until I draw blood or they cry out in pain. And that's about it for activity until day two, when this big gangly woman stops by. She's wearing jeans and she's got brown hair on her head and blond hair on her arms, so I figure she's a mixed breed. I'm leaning against the bars, biting her for as long as she can stand it—I'm getting very close to making a puncture wound—when I hear a lot of discussion, and the next thing I know, she springs me. She puts me on her lap and starts driving, which I know can't be very safe. At first I think maybe she's taking me to meet *Air Force One*. However, it begins to hit me that her car smells like dog vomit. Which makes me think she's not a Republican.

When we arrive at her house, right away I can't believe my eyes because *everywhere I look is a great place to go to the bathroom*!!! But already I'm thinking this woman has some serious mental problems, because every time I start to take a leak, she's in my face interrupting me. She's going, "No! No! No!" and trying to make me relocate *out in the yard*!!! I'm serious! In the dark! Or in the rain!!! Like it's the eleven hundreds. Suddenly I think I'm Olivia de Havilland in *The Snake Pit*.

The craziness doesn't end here. Now I find out that she doesn't want me to eat. I mean, I'm starving, I'm *teething*, and her place is like a big all-you-can-eat buffet. *Everywhere I look is edible stuff*. But when I try to take a mouthful she's in my face again. She doesn't want me to eat *anything*. Not clothes. Not nails. Not candles. Not door frames. Not *nothing*. It's like everything I know to be true about the world has suddenly shifted, and now every single idea that I have is a problem. As it happens, I've always prided myself on my original thinking. I'm an idea man. But suddenly this woman is telling me that *everything I do is wrong*.

I get the idea "Let's pull up the rug and eat the foam-rubber pad" and of course, no, we can't do that. So then I figure, "Let's eat all the wires wherever we find them attached to the wall," and that's no good. So then I think, "Let's find a pack of needles behind the bed and chew on them," and of course, there's something wrong with that too. And it doesn't even occur to her that the law of averages would dictate that *all* these ideas couldn't possibly be bad. That just maybe *she's* wrong occasionally.

Obviously, something else is going on here. I mean, it's more than a coincidence that she doesn't want me to pull up her plants *or* rip her upholstery *or* eat her books and magazines. It begins to dawn on me that I'm more than just a long, long way from the White House. I mean, not only do I not attend cabinet meetings, but I seem to be stuck in some kind of banana republic here, with her as the pack leader!! (And as far as I can tell, all she has in the way of qualifications is *height*.) It's not just the arbitrary restrictions; now when she leaves the house, she locks me up in the kitchen.

The first gate she puts up I can climb, no problem. Even though it's covered with wire mesh, I can just dead-drop to the floor. And so for at least that one brief shining moment I am actually able to accomplish things that I can point to with pride. For instance, by the time she gets home that day I've not only dismantled and consumed most of a telephone, but I've also eaten over half of the paperback *Toxic Parents: Overcoming Their Hurtful Legacy and Reclaiming Your Life.*

Let's just say she's not impressed by this. I don't think she gets the message I'm trying to send her, either. Instead of looking within, she just hires a guy to make the gate more difficult to climb! So now when she goes out, I have no choice but to sit in the kitchen alone, surrounded by mysterious squeaking vinyl food replicas. I don't understand the full implications of that pork chop, but I do know it's the toughest, noisiest piece of meat with which I have ever had the misfortune to be imprisoned.

By now I've realized that this woman and I have very little in common, also that we seem to have a completely different relationship to every single thing in the universe. Give you an example. She's sitting on the bed, doing nothing, with a lap full of newspapers. So I decide to take the edge of one section and run around with it and then sit on it and shred it into tiny fragments. This breakthrough idea meets with the kind of reactionary response that has plagued all forward-thinking individuals throughout history. Galileo and Leonardo and Newt Gingrich come to mind. Of course she's yelling "No! No! No!" like her way is the *only* way. Let's all just fill our laps with papers and *sit* there. It's no wonder her last two dogs had eating disorders.

And then there are the shots. Then more shots. I won't even tell you about them. It would sicken you. But at about week sixteen the shots suddenly end and the walks begin. This is my first opportunity to build some equity in the neighborhood. I realize right off it's a smart idea to acquire as much beachfront property as possible, what with the recession and everything. But what surprises me is the effortless way in which I am permitted to annex several impressive pieces of property, not the least of which is Johnny Carson's tennis compound—a several-acre island parcel off a cul-de-sac about a half mile from my central residence. It takes me only about two weeks of saturation peeing to take full title.

I admit to being a little surprised that Carson didn't put up any kind of a fight at all. On the other hand, I don't know how much he uses the place these days. There's mushrooms growing on the southeast corner and a dead bird just slightly west, which I have never seen him even try to roll on.

At about this point in the Barbara Bush book, there's a big kiss-ass section with photos of Millie mingling with important government officials and celebrities. I was going to include a section like that in here, but frankly I found the whole thing pathetic. Sure, I could name-drop. I just don't feel the need. Why should I try to make myself sound more important by telling you that last weekend at the dog park in Laurel Canyon I sniffed Julia Roberts's big fat black dog's butt?

No, I refuse to resort to that kind of nonsense, because I happen to believe that some things matter more than having your picture taken sitting with Secretary of State George Shultz and Her Majesty Queen Noor of Jordan. Or French president François Mitterrand and Mrs. Yasuhiro Nakasone. That's why I have decided to close by sharing with you a part of my credo, which I hope you will value and cherish as I do.

My Credo

If you like something well enough to climb on it or kiss it, then don't you also owe it to yourself to eat it or destroy it? Can't you at least take the time to pick it up in your mouth and run with it as fast as you can from room to room until it drops? Or shred it into microscopic particles?

Because as we wander through this world, I think it is important not to lose sight of this amazing truth: *Everything* is potentially an entrée, if not also a side dish or an hors d'oeuvre. If you look at things properly, you'll come to realize that there's no need to wait for the dessert cart. Dessert is *everywhere*. Thank you.

Look Before
You Eat

Only a woman under male surveillance will partake of quaint ceremonies like "dinnertime," featuring items from the major food groups arranged on a plate and served at a table. When a woman is alone and unobserved (and by *a woman* I of course mean me) she's likely to choose instead a supposedly calorie-conscious replacement for dinner: a couple of spoonfuls of yogurt at six o'clock, a few handfuls of dry shredded wheat or croutons at seven, a careful scanning of cupboards and refrigeration chambers at eight, followed by popcorn and pickle chips, wine or beers at ten, and eventually a giant saucepan full of barely heated refried beans just before bed. I haven't calculated the overall caloric intake of this activity, but I suspect it's probably just about double what any ordinary sane meal might provide.

Which brings me to a topic in which I, as a single woman, have achieved a certain unwilling expertise: eating out. This knowledge amounts to a short list of the particular signals that can tip you off to the inevitability of an overpriced, unsatisfying dining experience. I'm referring here to more subtle indicators than giant turquoise drinks garnished with parasols and served in ceramic whales—which actually can add a certain ironic hipness to the whole event that I find appealing. The following danger signals cannot serve in any ironic way whatsoever. Which is why I encourage you to memorize them as you would your Social Security number.

1. Signs Can Be Dangerous.

Exercise grave caution in the presence of any engraved wooden sign hanging outside the restaurant that uses words like "purveyors of" or "ye olde." The likelihood of anyone for miles around being from Merry Olde England is pretty slight. And stay away from any place that has a cute or excessively clever name—whether it involves a fictitious lovable curmudgeonly owner (like Señor Grumbley Wumbley or Dr. Munchies) or an adjective attached to an animal (like the Happy Hamster). This goes double for signs that show a cheery cartoon drawing of the animal dressed in a sailor suit dancing the hornpipe. Any restaurant that wants you to imagine your food having a great time on shore leave only moments before death does not deserve your patronage. Also to be avoided are restaurant names that suggest the food itself has a describable personality, like the Contented Carrot or the Good-Natured Potato. Maybe it's too obvious even to *mention* the n-apostrophe places, like Meat 'n' Wheat. But be afraid. Be very afraid.

2. Avoid Any Eating Establishment with a Visible Motif.

This means not only painted Grecian urns and fake antiquities, but lit torches, stagecoach parts, boat sections, pieces of driftwood, unattached wheels of all kinds, decorative remnants of air disasters, etc. I believe it is Newton's Third Law that tells us it's physically impossible for good food and fishnets full of glass balls to occupy the same space at the same time. Footnote: This particular rule applies only to places within a 100-mile radius of major metropolitan city limits. Once you have crossed that geographic barrier, it appears that decent family-style places can coexist quite nicely with out-of-season Christmas tree ornaments or preserved animal remains. Scientists are only now beginning to understand this phenomenon, so don't expect an explanation from me. Which leads directly to my next point, and perhaps my most puzzling:

3. A Place That Looks Like a Dump Doesn't Necessarily Serve Good Home Cooking.

All right. Having evaluated the exterior of the restaurant, it's time to step tentatively into the interior. We still have scrutinizing to do before we allow ourselves to be seated.

4. If the Seating in the Restaurant Is Anything Other Than Tables, Chairs, or Booths, Take a Hike.

Do not allow yourself to be seated on oldtime whiskey kegs, for example, or antique barrels or colorful containers of battery acid. Rattan peacock chairs, the kind that Huey P. Newton used to like being photographed in, are no exception to the rule, especially when accompanied by wooden ceiling fans or other *Casablanca*-style accessories.

5. Beware Too Much Wood.

Especially when it is pitched at a forty-five-degree angle. I can hear a lot of you resisting me on this one, claiming that wood provides a nice ambience. Be that as it may, it has been my experience that too much forty-five-degree-angle wood reveals less about décor than it does about the presence of walleyed teenage chefs playing Space Invaders with frozen food packets and a microwave.

6. Beware Multiple Dining Rooms.

Especially when accompanied by signs that say PARTY AND BANQUET FACILITIES or WE WELCOME TOUR BUSES. As a rule, anything (including blackened redfish) prepared in quantities of over one hundred portions at once turns into Beefaroni.

7. Beware No Other Customers.

This may not mean that you have stumbled upon a "find." The place has been found and then avoided by people with more sense than you will have if you stay.

8. Beware Colorful, Period-Style Uniforms.

"Olde English barmaids and wenches" are, of course, suspect, as are "cowpokes" and "pirates." And while the verdict's still out on "pouty European artistes," if you check with me in a year I will probably tell you that I always had a bad feeling about this ever-growing waitress motif.

At this point you may allow yourself to be seated, if you are not already so exhausted that you decide to give up. But do not place any sort of an order until you have carefully perused the menu for the following:

1. An Appropriate Degree of Menu-ness

By this is meant a piece of folded or laminated paper containing available meal selections and corresponding prices. The menu should not provide extra data about a historical period or culture that is supposed to trick you into thinking you are elsewhere. And it shouldn't be written on a rowboat oar or a dressmaker's dummy or hand-lettered on somebody's bare chest. Open the menu and promptly leave if you observe any of the following:

2. Use of the Phrase "Our Famous" or Worse, "Our World-Famous"

As seen in "our world-famous cheesecake" or "our world-famous salad bar." They not only never are, they can give you such serious pause for thought about the state of world fame that you can disappear into a searing depression for several weeks.

3. Repeated Use of Colorful Descriptive Words Such as "Zesty" or "Hearty"

Or colorful substitute nouns such as "grog" or "munchies" or "savories" or "victuals" or "libations." Or poetic renamings of the bland, as in "toast medley" or "vegetarian symphony."

4. Mixture of Cuisines That Makes No Sense

A new Mexican restaurant opened up in what I laughingly call my neighborhood. It serves quesadillas with pine nuts and goat cheese. It's the rare kitchen staff that knows how to cook *one* cuisine very well, let alone CUBAN FOOD AND MANDARIN CHINESE. Remember, you're safest where they have fewer things to screw up.

5. Any Menu That Indicates *I* Had Any Hand in the Food Preparations

This includes any invitation to dinner at my house. I don't want to be too specific, but I have had warnings from the Board of Health and am one of the few private citizens whose kitchen has been closed by law.

Well, there you have it. *Bon appétit.* You're on your own.

Dominatrix 101

The class description in the course catalog that I picked off the top of a pile on the floor of the frozen yogurt place asks a question that speaks to my very soul: "Do you want to learn how to make big money in a safe legal profession that will never leave you bored?" The answer is "Yes! Yes! A thousand times yes!"

That is just one of the reasons why I am among the fifty or sixty women of every race, body type, and demographic sample profile who are filing into the conference room on the top floor of that hallowed institution of higher learning—the Hyatt Hotel on Sunset Strip in the heart of Hollywood. On our way to our seats we all smile and say hello to a guy in a Hawaiian shirt. In short order our teacher, a blond woman of about fifty, appears at the front of the room. Dressed in a two-piece turquoise suit with a bright yellow blouse and sporting a short sensible haircut, she is almost unrecognizable from the shiny, leathery photo that she uses to advertise her class in the Learning Annex brochure. She is "Internationally Known Dominatrix Ava Taurel" and she is here to explain to us how to "Become a Dominatrix for Fun, Love and Profit." "Whether you want to enhance your relationships or become a professional dominatrix, this class will show you how." I find myself scrutinizing the perfectly random group of women around me, trying to guess who is here for which motive. It is impossible to tell.

"As you know, the class is for women only," Ava begins. "This upsets a lot of men. They have threatened to sue me for sex discrimination because they all want to come to the class. Right now they are hanging around down in the lobby, panting. But before we begin, I promised this one fellow he could speak with you for just a minute." The guy in the Hawaiian shirt steps forward. He tells us that he is a fitness trainer and a masseur and he just wants us to know that he is "available for whatever comes to mind so you can practice to be better dominatrixes." With that he distributes business cards to any interested takers and bids us a hearty farewell.

Now class is in session for real. To warm us up, Ava has spliced together a tape montage of famous scenes in the history of movies involving female domination: Susan Sarandon tying up Tim Robbins in *Bull Durham;* Melanie Griffith tying up Jeff Daniels in *Something Wild;* Sharon Stone in just about anything.

I find myself succumbing to my old school behavior patterns: tugging at my hair, shifting in my seat, glancing at my watch. However, it is only when Ava begins a free-form Q-and-A session that I realize I'm not in Comp. Lit. anymore.

The first question comes from a cute blond girl in her early twenties wearing a baseball cap who explains that she has just gotten her first real job at a dungeon and wants to know whether or not she should buy her own equipment.

"It varies from place to place," Ava tells her, "but before you do, make sure they have good lockers." Good lockers. Write that down.

Next a hugely obese lady wants to know how to get started in her own business. Ava cautions her about working outside of a protected environment, then explains how it is a good idea to operate from an office that overlooks a pay phone so that you can scrutinize a potential client before you take him on. That would apply to *all* walks of life. Write that down too.

From there Ava is off and running on a topic she knows well—what it takes to be a *good* dominatrix. "A wicked imagination," she begins. Mmmhmm. I have that. "And you must be able to give a clear command with your eyes. Sometimes they are steel. Sometimes they are caring." Still sounds doable. "It's very important to improvise," she points out. Hey! I'm good at improv! For example, Ava once had a man dress up as a maid, wear jingle bells on his testicles, and walk up and down the halls of his apartment house ten times. I raise my hand. I want to know what the best adhesive is for attaching the bells. But the woman in front of me gets called on first. She says that she had the idea of making a man chew on a bone. "Very nice," says Ava, clearly impressed. "You must develop your own uniqueness."

My own uniqueness. Sounds promising.

Fondly Ava recalls the golden days when she had ten women with different uniquenesses working for her. "For instance, one woman might not like pain but might be very skilled at verbal abuse." Well, I'm certainly verbal. "Then again. I remember a man who was into eating his own shit. *I* couldn't work with him. *I* would start throwing up. But for a woman who could stand it, it was three hundred dollars for fifteen minutes." Time to stop taking notes. Another misbegotten career right down the drain.

Now it is intermission, and not a moment too soon. All around me, networking breaks out. Gals are mingling around a table, writing down the titles on the reading list (*The Correct Sadist: Step by Step How to Turn a Man into a Slave*), perusing the new issue of *Rubber and Rivets.* (The cover story boasts, "Corsets aren't just for discipline anymore." Of course, I knew that.) "I'm a hypnotherapist and I teach a lot of mind games. You should give me a call," a distinguished-looking blonde in her early forties says to a plain pear-shaped woman in her early fifties.

When class resumes again, we meet another man. This one, a fit attractive guy in his forties, was *invited* by Ava. He drove over three hours from San Diego to volunteer his services. "He's a big strong man from the Navy Seals," says Ava, who orders him to take off his shirt and jacket before she will permit him to take questions from the group. An incredibly beautiful Asian woman raises her hand to ask a question. "Why don't you tell us about your background?" she requests. "Well, I'm from a small town in Pennsylvania," says the Seal. His dream was always to be a Navy Seal, he tells us, "chasing bad guys all over the world." He has many tales of manly danger. He wants us to know he has worked with explosives and high-powered weapons. He wants us to know that he has jumped out of planes and dived deep beneath the sea. He wants us to know about all this macho stuff so we can understand why he needs the release from stress that only wearing women's underwear can give him. I am puzzled. Wearing women's underwear has never helped me with stress.

I glance across the aisle from where I am sitting. The attractive black woman in the gray suit seated beside me has closed her eyes and dozed off for a second. But she is jolted back to consciousness when Mr. Navy Seal agrees to honor a request from the group to show us the red garter belt and white ladies' nylons that he is wearing under his pants. What a picture he makes. It's too bad the Navy Seals don't have one for their brochure. "Yes, I like being restrained," he admits as he lets his pants drop around his ankles. "I'm into erotic pain but I don't like my arms to be dismantled or anything like that."

"Just a few more questions," says Ava, "because I want us to start using him for different things. I want the women to take turns and come up one after the other." She lays out an assortment of whips, ropes, leashes, collars, and other dog accessories on a table nearby.

It starts out slowly at first. The large pear-shaped woman in the pink sweater asks him to kiss her hands. He does. Then it starts to heat up. A pretty blonde in tight jeans commands him to straddle a chair butt outward so she can practice her whipping technique. She smacks him tentatively. "Those pants are pretty thick. You can hit him harder," Ava advises. "You want to aim at the broad part of the back, or the back of the legs. You want to avoid this area here because you can hurt the kidneys." I raise my hand. I want to know if this will be on the final exam. The blonde smacks him much harder on her next try. Then she leans over to see his reaction. "He's smiling," she reports back to the class. "Make him say thank you!" a class member yells out. "Do you want some more?" the blonde asks him. "Yes," he mumbles. "I can't hear you," she taunts him. The class applauds spontaneously.

The next woman up to bat is a plain, boxy Latino woman in her early forties, dressed in a black-and-white-striped suit with a knee-length skirt. She commands the Navy Seal to get on his knees. "Kiss my feet," she orders. "That's it. I've been home all day and they do hurt. Take off my shoes and smell them. Oh? You think that's funny? Then put my leg between your thighs and hump it like the dog that you are." *And he does it.* Well, it *is* school. Maybe he's worried about his GPA. The class breaks out in applause again. I am thinking, *Who are these people?*

Whereupon a gorgeous white woman with long black hair and *enormous* breasts, dressed in a skin-tight red sweater and short black skirt, takes confident control of the Seal. She puts him into a dog collar, attaches it to a leash, and begins to lead him up and down the aisles. *Now* I'm angry. His leash technique is *sooo* much better than what I can get from *any* of my four dogs, even after all that expensive training. I can't take it anymore. This is the final insult!

"The lady who is leading him around the room is his wife," announces Ava. Happily reunited, the Seal and the babe take the stage and answer questions like they are a celebrity couple: The Liz and Larry Fortensky of Domination. "You never told me you like to be whipped," she teases. "He never liked to be whipped before."

"Really???" says the blonde who did the whipping, suddenly embarrassed and full of remorse. "I didn't know you didn't like to be whipped. Because I don't like to whip either. I guess I should have asked you first."

"Communication is very important," says Ava. "I guess we were both a little nervous," says the Seal. Everyone nods.

"Well, that's it for tonight," says Ava, "except for those of you who would like to work on knots." It's almost eleven P.M. I think I'll work on my knots in the morning.

On the way down in the elevator, a bunch of us compare notes. "It was either this or an antiques lecture. And the antiques lecture was sold out," says a very professorial-looking black woman, waving good-bye as we head across the parking lot to our individual cars.

Diary of a
New Relationship

I guess every man has an idealized image of the woman he loves. And my man apparently wants me to look like Nikki Sixx.

One of the unique and enduring qualities of this not-so-new-anymore relationship is the emphasis on hair fluffing. In past relationships, very little comment was made about my looks in general. No comment was ever made about the fluffiness level of my hair.

In my past romantic entanglements, most of what I did in the name of vanity was discouraged, or simply not acknowledged at all. When I wore eye shadow, one long-term boyfriend used to fix me with a withering glance and say, "Why do you have green stuff on your eyelids?" As if there might be a good answer to that, like "What? Are you serious? Let me get this straight. You're saying there's green stuff on my eyelids?" Or perhaps the more technical "Well, I'm suffering from eyelid fungus."

Of course, that particular former member of my roster of

so-called serious boyfriends once took off his Hawaiian shirt and cleaned his windshield with it, then put it back on and went out to dinner. When that is taken into account, it is not so surprising that the fluffiness of my hair was not one of his concerns.

But now I have a boyfriend who is a musician. And he, like others of his kind, puts a lot of emphasis on image. He looks at those scary pictures of Mötley Crüe in their platform boots and spandex pants from the eighties and thinks, "Wow. Great hair."

His effect on my overall appearance has been such that right now, as I write this, my hair is a full 75 percent fluffier than at any previous point in my history. But then again, I come from the Joni Mitchell sleek-and-wounded-too-artistic for-hair-product tradition. Perhaps that is why I am still not certain that fluffiness is a look I can pull off. Not everyone can do everything. Donald Rumsfeld, for instance, will never be thought of as a punk. Pamela Anderson will not be confused with an academician. And so, too, I have found that there are certain adjectives and looks that no one has ever used when describing me. "Delicate," "dainty," "tidy," and "petite" are some of them, along with "Gladiator," "Bank President," "Race Car Driver," and "Supermodel." "Fluffy" has always been on all such lists.

Because I am in love with my current boyfriend, I try to do what I can to please him. But when I catch a glimpse of myself in a store window, I never fail to worry that the fluffier my hair gets, the less I look like Pink and the more I look like Madeleine Albright in a party dress. I fear that I look like I am trying too hard and failing miserably. Like a bulldog fresh from the groomer who is still wearing a bow.

Some of this stems from the difference between being a writer and being a musician.

Musicians strut. They are peacocks. When they look around the world for role models, they think flash. They think Keith Richards and David Bowie. They pose for album covers bare-chested, wearing only a truss, lime green bell-bottoms, and a fedora.

Writers skulk. They stare, unsmiling, deadpan and miserable, from their book jacket photos. Writers attract attention at parties by looking away when you look at them so they will never look like they care if you look or not. Even though they know that you are and like that you are and hope you will keep looking so they can keep looking away when you do. When I survey this parched landscape for role models, I feel lucky if I can pull off Joyce Carol Oates.

The boyfriend does not understand, no matter how hard I try to explain, what it means to have tried and failed with big ratted hair for decades. When I was in junior high, everyone I hung out with could knock low branches off trees with their pyramids of cantilevered hair. They carried cans of hair spray the size of scuba tanks in their purses for on-the-spot maintenance between classes. Hoping to blend in, I, too, would spend all five of the allotted minutes between classes ratting and spraying my hair into a big bubble. But once I left the spraying chamber and returned to the classroom, amid the people I hoped to impress, my hair would deflate like an inadequately prepared pan of Jiffy Pop. Flat and sad, it lay on my head rigid and mangled like a drugged animal; I could almost hear the air escaping the way it does from a punctured balloon. "Fuck you. You can't tell me what to do, asshole," my teenage hair would yell at me.

But the new boyfriend cannot really comprehend my dilemma. The new boyfriend comes to me complete with a history of previous girlfriends who were all winners in the Vanity Derby. I refer here to the kind of rock-and-roll bohemian girls with hair the color of nail polish who can assemble a fetching outfit by throwing together a hula skirt, a mohair sweater, a mattress cover, a prayer shawl, and oven mitts. Some were women who worked as exotic dancers and therefore spent as much time fixing their lip liner and pasting on eyelashes as I spend cleaning up dog shit.

In other words, a *lot* of time.

Insecurities aside, I still feel that the new boyfriend is a step in the right direction, because I am at long last following the advice of my mother, who harped at me, from early childhood on, "Stop running around with all those worthless lawyers and accountants and settle down with a nice rock musician."

My parents were very critical people, who felt that their mission in life was to protect me from the stress that having a shred of self-esteem might cause me. In their eyes I was always too fat or too thin, I was wearing too much makeup or not enough. For me to have been the kind of daughter my parents had in mind, I should have been born with an Etch A Sketch for a face.

Therefore, my current hair dilemma with the new beau fits neatly into what my shrink calls repetition compulsion. My mother also complained ad nauseam about my hair. However, she had a different solution. Her mantra was always "Get your hair out of your face"—the better to see the sunshine reflecting off my big beaming forehead like a spotlight on a newly arriving space alien.

Whereas "Get your hair into your face" is the mantra of

the new boyfriend. "Did you cut your bangs?" is often the first thing he says to me when I greet him at the door.

"Well, yes. Because *I can't see.*"

"So you can't see," he will say. "You'll get used to it." And the next thing I know, he is headed toward me, his hands reaching forward, fingers extended in the fluffing position.

In the name of helping this all along, I have purchased at least one bottle of every volumizer product currently for sale. Sadly, these preparations do not create volume, but rather are more like Viagra in that they produce a kind of stiffness that only lasts for about an hour.

So I don't know what the answer is.

Wigs are too hot. And hats blow off. The only thing I can think of that gives me hope is that if this relationship really lasts, the way I am hoping it will, in the fullness of time his eyesight is sure to deteriorate. Then perhaps I can convince him that my hair is in fact really fluffy. It's the prescription in his glasses that is the problem.

Home Alone

The other night I ate a pack of frozen hors d'oeuvres for dinner: three weenie rolls, two egg rolls, three potato puffs, and three air-filled triangular things. When I confided this information to a friend, she remarked, "Well, that's the kind of thing you can do only when your life is completely unobserved."

This is the first extended period of time that I have lived alone. By "alone" I mean without humans, because, except for a few weeks, I have always had dogs (and dogs are no help at all when it comes to goofy behavior; in most instances they only encourage it). Which brings me to my point: When you live alone you are apt to turn into the silliest version of yourself, simply because there is no one around to stop you.

When you live with your parents, you are expected to play by their rules, no matter how hip or evolved your folks might pretend to be. And when you live with a man—I don't need to tell you how it works when you live with a man, do I? After a lifetime of living both with parents and with men, I am only too well acquainted with what have erroneously been referred to as my "annoying habits." The question is, Are your habits still annoying if there is no one around to say he or she is pissed off? And of course the answer comes back a resounding "No! No! A thousand times no!" It's just like magic. When you live by yourself, all your annoying habits are *gone*!!

Which is not to say that living alone is something to strive for. Quite frankly, several things about it are not too appealing. It can be lonely and boring. There's no one around to whine to. Plus, you have to lift those enormous containers of bottled water all by yourself. I once stayed in a relationship almost a year past its due date just to avoid confronting the issue of the giant bottles of water.

The good part is that these circumstances force you to learn to do stuff you might otherwise have avoided entirely, like finding out where the circuit breakers are and how to turn off the water at its source. Or how to eat alone in a restaurant without making a face that continuously says, "The person who is meeting me here should have been here by now. I wonder what in the world is causing the delay!"

When you live alone you find yourself getting both very brave and very stupid. There's no one to comment when you play one cut from an album 300 times in a row. Or rent a movie and replay it during the cute guys. You can go *whole days* without turning the television on at all (cheerfully ignoring those important hours of stock-car racing from Daytona!). Finally, there's the real plus: When you live by yourself you don't have to worry that you're not getting enough fats and sugars in your diet.

The bad part is that it's possible, by indulging your whims, to turn into a caricature of yourself. There is a point at which the good side of living alone and the bad side of living alone converge. For instance, one of the good things is that you can relax and spend the whole day looking like a pig if you want to. And one of the bad things is that you can catch a glimpse of yourself in the mirror and realize that you have just spent the whole day looking like a pig. This is a phenomenon I call the Fish Table Principle, so named because when you live by yourself, you can go ahead and buy a table that looks like a fish without fear of reprisal. But then you have to go through life pretending to enjoy living with a table that looks like a fish.

So we see that this whole living-alone business is a mixed bag. But having done it for the past couple of years, I feel I must caution the neophyte to avoid one danger area right from the start. I refer to the reading of articles in women's magazines, like *Cosmopolitan,* that purport to give advice on living by yourself with flair. They almost always involve "pampering yourself," which generally boils down to "Treat yourself to a bubble bath!" Then there's the old "cooking a fabulous dinner for one, using the good china and the good silver" technique. (Right away making the dangerous assumption that you may have some of each.)

When I first started living alone, I used to scour these articles. Quickly they became a source of real irritation. The truth is that a lot of women end up living alone as a result of troublesome circumstances. These women, like me, have quite enough to worry about without the added stress of feeling they're not executing their daily rituals with sufficient style to please Helen Gurley Brown. So, let the *Cosmo* women lightly braise their short ribs and toss up a celeriac vinaigrette for one. Here are my alternative suggestions for the flakier, lazier woman who doesn't want to go to the store because it's too cold (or too hot) and anyway there's still half a box of Wheat Thins and a couple of beers in the fridge.

Merrill Presents Eight Things to Do When You Are Living Alone, Because Now There Is No One to Stop You

1. Dye your hair a lot of exotic colors that always fascinated you but you were too chicken to try. Then cut it all off, buy a really big hat, walk up to randomly selected people on the street, glare at them, and say ferociously, "What exactly are you staring at?"
2. See if you can eat a full three-course dinner in your car before even leaving the supermarket parking lot. Be sure to use the good silver.
3. Test really unusual clothes for falling asleep in. While you're at it, why not try sleeping on a different edge of the bed every night?
4. Shave the dog, oil him, then sit next to him out in the yard and see who gets a good all-over tan first.
5. Take yourself out on a date! Make reservations at your favorite restaurant. At the table, try moving back and forth between two chairs as you find out where you're from and what your major was in college. Afterward, if you feel there's too much pressure on you to go right to bed, take out a can of Mace and spray yourself thoroughly.
6. One night cook yourself a dinner that includes lean meat/fish/poultry, leafy green or yellow vegetables, and a starch!

7. Call up a radio psychologist under the pretense of needing some help, and when he or she says, "Turn your radio down," turn it *up*!

8. Call to get an appointment with the phone repair guy or someone from the gas or electric company. When they ask, "Will someone be home between eight A.M. and ten P.M.?" reply, "No, I live by myself and I work for a living. I can't be there for fourteen hours in a row." When they begin to tell you that they're sorry, they're very sorry, but unless someone is there from 8:00 A.M. to 10:00 P.M. there's nothing they can do to help you, tell them to please hold. Drive quickly to their place of employment, find them, and threaten them with bodily harm from a blunt instrument. At your trial insist that "a jury of my peers" means "other single people who live alone." You'll be cleared of all charges and home playing the same cut on the album 300 times in a row in no time flat.

My Romantic Dinner with Fabio

Monday morning the sun staggered sleepily through the grimy blinds of my vine-covered Malibu bungalow as I awakened to the sounds of a ringing telephone. Lazily I stretched out my long tanned limbs like a tawny lynx as I struggled to answer it, reaching over the four sleeping dogs between me and the nightstand. It was a woman from *TV Guide*. "We would like you to write an article entitled 'My Romantic Dinner with Fabio,'" she said. My tender lips trembled as I silently mouthed the words. "My Romantic Dinner with Fabio??" I shook my tousled mane of raven hair as I tried to comprehend the idea of me and Fabio ever, even momentarily, sharing the same breathing space on the planet. Until now, it had seemed just a shade less likely than a surprise announcement that I had been appointed the new replacement for Donald Rumsfield. "Yes, okay. I'll do it," I heard myself whisper. "His people will call you," she replied. "They would like to do it on Wednesday."

Within hours I was on the phone with Peter Paul, Fabio's manager. He was anxious to tell me about "Fabio's message of support for the rights and needs of women." Plus his new video, his newly renovated international 900 number, his perfume endorsement, and his future plans to make action-adventure movies with video game merchandising and Marvel comics tie-ins. My pale hands began to tremble as I realized that for the first time in my life my bosom was starting to heave.

Tuesday

I arise bright and early and head off to the store to purchase *Pirate,* the romance novel that Fabio sort of wrote. As I inspect the only cover photo I have ever seen of an author scowling, bare-chested, and wielding a scabbard (except, of course, for the one of Eudora Welty) I cannot help feeling a pang of envy at the way my companion-to-be has achieved a career as a bestselling author without having to suffer the fatigue, torture, and endless irritations of actually having to sit down and write. If only he will share his secrets with me.

By the time I get home, his press kit has arrived and soon I am awash in articles about Fabio published in every imaginable publication, as well, of course, as thousands of vivid color photographs. Fabio, astride a motorcycle, bare-chested and scowling. Fabio, holding a bouquet of roses, dressed only in tuxedo pants and suspenders, scowling as he heads out the door to the world's most casual black-tie event. The anticipation is building. *Yes, yes,* I think to myself. *I have dined before with many scowling guys. But always in the past they were wearing two or more shirts.*

Wednesday

I spend the day consumed with but a single thought: What exactly is the appropriate attire to wear to a romantic dinner with Fabio? I try on millions of outfits, unsure of what I am even after. Perhaps it's the name that's so intimidating. Maybe if I think of him as "Ricky." Then I only have to answer the question, "What do I wear out to dinner with Ricky?" Much much more doable.

I have been told a limousine will pick me up at 6:45. By then my bosom is heaving so hard, I tuck some smelling salts in my purse. Eagerly I watch as the clock turns to 6:45, then 7:00, then 7:10. By 7:15 I am beginning to accumulate a light sprinkling of dog hairs. One dog has placed a filthy sock full of tennis balls on my lap, another has started a small snag in my pantyhose. Undaunted, I continue to wait breathlessly. But alas . . . by 7:30 I grow concerned. Mayhap he has been waylaid by danger? I daren't phone his people for fear he will chortle scornfully and call me "a demanding little minx" like he did the girl in his book. So instead, I relax, take off my jacket, and fix myself half a toasted bagel.

By 7:45 I am beginning to doze when I am awakened by the plaintive howls of my dogs. Hastily I re-dress and run to peer out my front window. The gate opens and . . . a limousine driver just stands there, holding my front gate open. When he keeps on just standing there, I grab my purse and head out the door. And behold! Out in my driveway: a limousine full of Fabio. When I realize this is part of the ancient Buccaneer custom of "waiting for the woman out in the car but also bringing *two* beautiful bouquets of yellow roses to distract her so she won't be pissed." I am appeased. Plus, there is another special surprise just for me. Fabio is wearing a shirt! A red cotton pullover with a V-neck zipper, under a blue-gray sport coat. I am deeply, deeply relieved. We say hello. Our eyes meet and . . . yep. My new friend Ricky looks just exactly like Fabio.

The limo whisks us off to Geoffrey's, one of the prettiest restaurants on the Malibu coast. Although I have been there many many times before, this is the only visit at which the entire female staff turned out to give us a tour. We are seated at a lovely veranda table with a view of the whole coast at night. The nearby heat lamp casts a golden glow on our powerful bodies. I ask him to tell me about his dogs, one of the things I know we have in common. His face lights up as he speaks fondly of his three purebred 175-pound Great Danes, one of which is on a list of "The 22 Most Beautiful Animals in the World." I have never seen this list, so I do not know if any of my dogs made it. Nevertheless, we begin to bond on the topic of dog-related damage. "Oh yeah, nose prints," he tells me. "The house have a lot of door windows and they have the nose prints all over. The house where I was staying, they almost chew through a wall," he confides. "I am screaming at them when I catch them and they look at me like 'I didn't do anything.' Except they are covered with white stuff on their big black noses from where they eat the wall." He laughs bravely through his tears. "It's a beautiful thing because they give unconditional love. Very hard to find."

The waiter arrives and Fabio orders oysters on the half shell. I order a Caesar salad. "You're not a vegetarian, are you?" he asks. "I don't want you to turn into a cucumber." Our eyes meet again as I take out a pile of his publicity photos. "This guy lying facedown in the pounding surf, bare-chested and scowling," I say to him, "what is he thinking to himself when he poses like this?"

"He is saying 'I am ready to seduce you. Let me be your man. Let me make you feel like a real woman,' " he tells me.

"How about, 'Let me come into your life and get wet sand all over your furniture?' " I suggest.

He grins at me as he eats an oyster. "You are funny girl," he says. "Bon appetite."

As we dine on pasta with shiitake mushrooms (or "shtucky mushrooms" as Fabio calls them) we speak of many things. His hopes: "I want to create a new superhero that appeals to men AND women. Schwarzenegger appeals only to men." His dreams: "When you branch yourself out as a business person you see many opportunities." "So will we one day awaken to see 'Fabio's House of Pancakes?' " I ask. "Well, I like food," he replies. "But I would do healthy stuff. Shakes and omelettes." The difficulties men and women have communicating: "People don't say anything honest to each other," he says wistfully. "People like to play games. I don't like to play games. I don't want to play games. I hate to play games." "What *kind* of games exactly?" I ask as I quietly push the Parcheesi board to the back of my purse where it will not upset him. "Mind games," he replies, "like when you see that a person really likes you and she plays very hard to get. I don't like that," he says, as he graciously accepts the rest of my dinner.

My bosom is heaving, my trachea engorged with partially swallowed pasta, as I decide it is time to find out just who *is* this man they call Fabio?

"Tell me," I say as he gazes into my upturned face, "what

would you do if you kissed a woman and she slobbered on you?"

"Nothing turns me off about a woman," he replies.

"What would happen if you looked over at me and I had just dropped a huge forkful of pasta onto my lap?" I rally.

"I would eat it," he laughs. I hope he likes pasta with dog hair, I think to myself.

"What if you were making out and a woman's stomach started to rumble?" I continue.

"I will try and get her a Pepto-Bismol," he says.

"And what if you went to her house and were making love and you found there were crumbs in her bed?"

"No big deal," he answers. "I block out. I don't pay attention."

Things are moving very fast. There is still one question unanswered. "What if she got drunk and threw up on you?" I ask breathlessly, the wind in my hair.

"Well, that's heavy," he admits. "I guess I go to the bathroom and try to clean up as best I can.

"Let me esplain you something," he says, as the gentle breeze blows softly through the remaining pasta. "Life is very easy. People complicates their life."

"I think life is kind of difficult," I confess.

"You make your life difficult," he tells me. "Probably you didn't let anybody at your same level come into your life. When somebody is equal, nobody has control. When you want to have control, the person you let come into your life is not gonna be your equal. The best feeling in love is to surrender to the other person."

Then he drops the bombshell that will change our future forever. "Now I have a person I spend time with. I'm really crazy about this person," he says. "She's a model-actress, extremely attractive, has a super super personality."

Okay, I accept that she is super times two, but what does he *see* in her? my heart cries out in the night. "How long has this been going on?" I ask quietly.

"A month," he tells me. "We have a great time and we are friends. We really don't want to rush. People always rush to make love."

"So the relationship hasn't been consummated yet?" I ask, thinking this may be more information than I need.

"We have time," he tells me. "Women sometime they rush and for the man it doesn't mean anything. What me and this person did is we know each other well first."

I sigh deeply as I gaze mournfully through the pain, past the piece of lettuce that is resting on my knee, off into the depths of the deep blue sea. And I recall the words he spoke to me back then: "The dogs no inside the house." I should have known then that we could never be.

And so we went our separate ways—he back to his life of publicity tours and business opportunities, and I back to my house full of dog-hair wads the size of a man's toupee. But late at night, whenever the gentle breeze blows through the pasta, I will remember the greatest love that never was. I will remember.

What the Dogs
Have Taught Me

Daily Routine

The day is divided into two important sections. *Mealtime.* And *everything else.*

I. Mealtime

1. Just because there does not seem to be anything *visible* around to eat certainly does not mean there is *nothing* around to eat. The act of staring at the underside of a table or chair on which someone else is eating sets in motion a chain of events that eventually results in food.
2. It goes without saying that you should carefully check the lower third of *any* space for edibles. Mouth-size things which cannot be identified by sight or smell are considered gum.
3. When you actually receive a meal, submerge your head into it as you would a shower. *Never, ever* look up again

until a minimum of at least fifteen minutes after the obvious food is gone. This is important. Just because your dish is empty does not mean that it is time to stop eating.

4. Remember that *all* food is potentially yours up until the time that it is actually swallowed by another. The lengthy path a piece of food will take from a plate to a mouth via a hand is as good a time as any to stake your claim to it.

5. When it comes to selecting an appropriate beverage, location and packaging mean *nothing*. There are *absolutely no exceptions* to this rule.

6. If you really see something you want, and all your other attempts at getting it have failed, it is only right to grovel shamelessly. As a second tactic, stare intently at the object of your desire, allowing long gelatinous drools to leak like icicles from your lower lip.

II. Everything Else

1. There are really only two important facial expressions to bother with: *complete overwhelming joy* and *nothing at all*.

2. Any time that is not mealtime is potentially nap time. The best time to take a nap is when you hear your name being called repeatedly. The best location for a nap is dead center of any street or driveway. The most relaxing position is on your side, all four limbs parallel.

3. The most practical way to get dry is to shake violently near a fully clothed person. A second effective method is to stand on a light-colored piece of furniture.

4. *Personal Security*

   A. At the first hint of any irregular noise, run from room to room yelling loudly. If someone actually comes into the house, rush over to them whether you know them or not. Then kiss them so violently that they lose their balance or have to force you away physically.

B. The greatest unacknowledged threat to life as we have come to know it is squirrels. No matter what you must do, make sure there are none in your yard.

5. *Recreation and Leisure*

A. *Ball:* No matter where you find them, in a bed or in a bathtub, no matter how they are dressed or how they behave, there is no such thing as a person who does not want to play ball all the time. There are two equally amusing sets of rules you will want to know.

   a. *The common form,* in which you receive a thrown ball and return it.

   b. *The preferred form,* in which you receive a thrown ball and eat it.

B. *Car:* As you know, any open car door is an invitation to get in. Once inside, your only goal is to try to get out.

6. *Health*

A. In the event of a trip to the doctor, always be on your guard. If you are vaccinated, urinate on the physician.

Afterword

Since I have taken to sleeping under the bed, I have come to know tranquillity I never imagined possible.

You never really know when it might be cookie time. And that's what the dogs have taught me.

My New Career
in Porn

"**Did you know** the adult-entertainment business is a billion-dollar industry that makes up to 65% of all money generated on the Internet?" was the question being asked in bold type under the headline for a class called "How to Make $$ in the Adult Entertainment Business on the Net." "Remember the ONLY business making money on the Internet is the Adult Entertainment Business," the course description went on to say. "The demand is great and there's no end in sight."

Like most Americans, I've kind of gotten used to the idea that no matter how sophisticated the new technology, the most successful application of it in the United States is going to be in the field of pornography. It isn't going to surprise me at all when the first retail business on the moon turns out to be an adult video store.

"There are people making a lot of money with adult sites—and so can you!" the ad went on to say. *This* was the part that surprised me. I had never, for even one second, thought of myself as a possible Internet pornmeister.

Of course, I had given a little thought as to how I might make the millions on the Internet that appear to be my constitutional birthright as a citizen in the year 2000. Was Internet porn the cash cow of which I had dreamed?

Deciding to familiarize myself with my new field by paying a visit to "VIRTUAL SIN: the wildly popular adult web site" run by my prospective teacher, Phillip LeMarque, I find myself looking at a large photo montage of sexually preoccupied women that looked as if it had been assembled out of old *Penthouse* magazines. Beneath it, a menu offered, among other things, "This week's story: A dick is a dick by Dick and Son," which turned out to be a series of captioned photographs of people having sex that were shot in motel rooms and some kind of garage, at enough of a distance to make them not particularly erotic or even all that visible. Their unique distinguishing feature was that each one contained an oddly phrased, poorly spelled caption balloon making the people having sex appear to be speaking English as a second language. For example, a man with a naked woman kneeling before him had the caption "A little enth*ousi*asm could do marvel around here."

And to think that the genius behind this was offering to share his wisdom with me! Which is why it was so odd that when the day actually arrived, I was feeling uneasy about attending the class. I practically wept with joy when my friend Susan said she would go along. Although I don't think she was all that comfortable, either, judging by the prayer she spoke aloud as we walked into the vagina-colored main building of the Radisson Hotel in Culver City, where the class was to be held. "Dear God," she said, "please don't let them go around the room and ask us to say our names. Amen."

We were both delighted when no one bothered to look up as we took seats in the very back of a third-floor conference room, near a long, skirted table laden with at least fifteen separate half-full pitchers of cold water. This adult website business apparently can make a person very thirsty!

There wasn't a lot of bonding going on among the nineteen people spread out over eight rows of oval-backed hotel-room chairs. All were staring with rapt attention at our instructor, Mr. English-as-a-Second-Language himself, a short, fire-hydrant-shaped gentleman with longish black and gray hair, wearing a maroon shirt over a white T-shirt tucked into gray-green cotton pants. He spoke with the kind of French accent that makes a sentence sound like this: "Technology is moving faster than we spick."

"It's a good time to get involved with the adult business," he was saying as we sat down. "Video strimming is esploding."

A little enthousiasm could do marvel around here, I thought to myself.

"What kind of a name are we gonna give our website?" he turned and asked the class, answering before anyone had a chance to get creative. "Let's say we are gonna call our site 'Mydickhorny dot com.' So now what we gotta do is get a server to host our site."

Surveying my fellow pornmeisters, I noticed that they seemed to fall into a few general categories: an Asian contingent of two, both male and wearing glasses and plaid shirts, seated on opposite sides of the room; five white twentysomething males with pale skin and brown hair that featured strangely short fringe-y bangs, all wearing blue shirts; two plain-faced blond women in denim, one of whom had a fishing rod; three ratty-haired heavily made-up fortysomething women all in black. The rest of the men looked like steakhouse maître d's with the exception of the guy in front of me, who had kind of a creepy Bernhard Goetz vibe, not helped at all by the fact that he wore abnormally thin white socks with his discount running shoes.

"We produce nothing, put it together in a nice package, and we make money while we sleep," our instructor explained, defining the complex tasks we have come here to study this evening. "But you are going to need five thousand dollars to invest for this to work. We are also going to need bandwith. About five to seven gigabytes a month is good. If the files are compressed properly you can probably get six or seven thousand hits a month. It's going to be about eight months until you make any money."

He seems to know a great many specific statistics. "A person has to see a thing nine times before it registers, before they react," he says, though he doesn't say where he learned this and no one bothers to ask.

"Now, what are you going to sell?" he asks, answering before anyone in class can start to suggest things. "You have to have an identity. You have to *be* somebody particular. You need to be straight, sadomasochist, something. You needs content. Not shitty stuff, either."

"You have to have your own specialty," pipes up one of the brown-haired twentysomethings who, it turns out, likes to raise his hand and state the obvious.

I ponder briefly what will make my site special. Is there an area of porn that hasn't been done yet? I am contemplating the idea of naked people with terrible head colds (you click on a blonde in a suggestive pose and she says, "I have a nasty sinus infection") when I notice that for the first time the class has sort of come to life. They love suggesting examples of specialty sex.

"Foot fetish," says one. "Lesbian," says another. "Some people like huge people," says one of the sunburned blondes in denim. A twentysomething knows a guy who makes $60,000 a month displaying pictures of underpants.

"Yes, exactly. And all kinds of ethnic groups are doing good right now," says the instructor. "The Spanish are coming up very strong. The Asian people have always been popular. You also have the Big Babies—the guys who wear the diapers. And the baby boomer is getting old, so now we can recycle Grandma! A guy I knows does very well with the women after sixty!" He pauses for dramatic effect. *"But you better know your specialty,"* he warns us. "If you yourself are not a homosexual, how you going to know what the hell they want? Like the people who shits on each other." He pauses again, making a face to let us know he is not among them. "This is not my thing," he continues diplomatically, "but these sells for eight hundred dollars. Just another avenue that maybe you want to think about."

Yes, there is much to think about. The creative possibilities are apparently limitless in the world of Internet porn. Although it turns out there is one area to avoid totally: "Do not show pictures of your girlfriend," our expert says emphatically. "Everyone who has done that is in trouble. They get sued. It just never works." I heave a giant sigh of relief on behalf of girlfriends everywhere.

"You have to know your market, do your research," he reiterates. "If your site is sadomasochist, you're gonna sell a lot of shackles. But if you don't know your area . . . well . . ." He shrugs, growing wistful as he recalls the guy who put up a bondage site but failed to do sufficient research. "He got the knots and ties all wrong, and ooh, it was a big mess. All the bondage people were mad as hell and complaining."

That this didn't have to happen is the point he is trying to make. There is, after all, a special bondage consultant you can hire for $4,000 a day who dresses in a little checkered school-girl outfit and will guarantee your knots are of the finest quality.

"It's like opening up a restaurant," our instructor says casually, for the first of five times this evening. "You have to listen to your clients when you make up your menu. They gonna tell you about what they want. You are in business to serve your client. Who here is their own content? Anyone?"

A pockmarked, goateed guy in a red shirt with the sleeves cut off and a red cap with sunglasses balancing on top of it raises his hand.

"Especially for you who is your own content," the instructor repeats. "In another class I have a girl who is her own content. She got a request that somebody want to see her naked by the refrigerator eating a banana. So she do it. Set up a guest book where they can tell you what they want."

"I'll do anything. I don't give a shit," says Redcap, taking the title, in that moment, of Scariest Guy in the Class.

"People on the Internet wants instant gratification," our instructor cautions as he prepares to share one of his fiendishly clever trade secrets. "You have ten seconds to sell them something. That is the reason we make our video clips only one and a half minutes long!" he confides, craftily. "Because when a guy starts to jerk off, and the clip ends, he has no choice but to buy some more! You see?"

Using our restaurant analogy, it would be like serving the

customer an unusually small hamburger. Which, come to think of it, worked pretty well for McDonald's.

One of the blondes raises her hand. "How many pictures do we need? Twenty? Fifty? Two thousand?"

"We're getting to that," the instructor tells us. "It's illegal to use someone else's pictures. How do you enforce that? It's impossible! But remember, you can take the same ass, just put different heads on them."

But there is more to the assembling of a good website than just the same old asses with an array of new faces.

"All kinds of links you can have," he tells us, showcasing just how diverse a pornographer can really be. "I just finished doing the site for the ultimate masturbating machine. Costs nine hundred thirty-five dollars, delivered. This machine will suck the dick. It's incredible! I put my fingers in it only and I'm going to buy it! You can put a banner for it up on your site," he suggests. "Sturdy, portable, and disposable" is how it is described in a brochure he passes around. "A hygienic substitute for sexual intercourse."

"Or you find stuff at the sex shows, the electronic shows. Go look around Chinatown. The Chinese are very good for this stuff." Case in point. "I know a guy who packages Velcro straps that you put around your dick. He is calling it the new Viagra! The guy makes two, three thousand bucks a month."

Yes. The ever expanding world of future porn holds more riches than small minds like mine can presently imagine. "You will be able to take a dildo, we put some ceramic sensor on it, you have the reverse sensor on his dick and boom—she can make love to twenty thousand men at the same time. This is here," he says blithely, barely acknowledging the magnitude of the dream he is providing for women everywhere. What little girl doesn't grow up hoping to live in a world where she will be able to make love to 20,000 men at once and not even have to cook a single one of them breakfast?

On this inspirational note, it is time for a break. I join the people gathered around the table at the front of the room to look at the samples he has brought with him: a disembodied breast made of spongy material with advertising printed on it; a magazine offering advice on the basics of flogging that contains a photo of a nude woman suspended in midair, not unlike Keanu Reeves in *The Matrix*. Someone clearly ponied up the $4,000 to bring in a bondage consultant. Those knots certainly appear to be correctly executed.

As the class begins to wrap up, we learn a lot of brass-tacks basics, like how to list your site with the twenty best search engines by putting a lot of keywords after your metatag. For instance: "fuck," "ass," "cunt," "blowjobs," "homosexuals," and "fetishism" will get us a lot of coverage from web browsers.

"We have a major problem," he tells us finally, "to get paid on the Internet. The credit card is the only way you are going to get paid.

"How many of you are worried about your privacy?"

I proudly hold up my hand.

"Don't worry about it. Forget it. Sleep tight. It's all over thirty years ago," he says. "The French, the Germans, the English, the U.S., the Australians all have a relationship to spy on each other."

Now we get to the real point of all this: He, Phillip Le-Marque, owner of the wildly popular website Virtual Sin, can be our server for $35 a month. He can give us bandwidth for $7 a giga. He can get us a $495 site already set up with the links to make money—links to Amsterdam, a chat room, a toy store—*plus* supply us with sixty good pictures. (And that's *before* we start to switch heads and the asses around.) We only need to make an initial investment of $6,700 to get ourselves going, up $1,700 from the first estimate of $5,000 earlier in the evening.

Well, I think to myself as we all head toward the elevator, I'll bear that in mind. Maybe instead of naked people with head colds, I will use myself as my content. I will sit in front of a camera in my underwear, and when customers make their requests I will tell them why I think they are nuts for even being there. People will pay to be insulted by the grouchy naked woman. Kind of the way they love those rude N.Y. deli waitresses.

And if that doesn't make me the Internet millions that are rightfully mine, maybe I'll try the same thing using someone else's head or ass.

It's a
Wonderful Lewis

It was a dark, damp, wintry evening when Lewis wandered out alone onto the dark, damp, rickety Malibu pier. He had not announced his departure, just vanished through a hole of his own construction in the front fence. In the process his collar had come off . . . name tag, rabies tag, everything. He was untraceable now. Simply gone. History.

He just could no longer think of a valid reason to stay. Scheduled dining was over for the evening, leaving no hope for another meal until the next day. Unless Merrill held one of those spontaneous snack times. Which she frequently did.

He guessed he could have hung around and stared at her mournfully, allowing long rubbery drools to coagulate in the corners of his lips. That seemed to encourage her some of the time. But not all of the time. Maybe that was what finally drove him to leave. This powerful inconsistent reinforcement was making him insane. He knew he had to get out of there.

Alone, looking down at the waves as they crashed, Lewis was suddenly overcome by the smell of . . . was that food? It beckoned him. "Lewis. Lewis. Come." A wrapper floated by in the murky deep. That was it. He poised himself for a dive.

Just then he became aware of a ghostly presence. Or perhaps it was an angelic one. He had never really absorbed enough television to know the difference. It seemed to have materialized out of a flash of light in the sky. So, unless it was a fly of some kind . . . hmmm, maybe it was a fly. He began to snap at it. But before he could secure it between his teeth, it began to speak.

"Hello, Lewis," the angelic presence said to him. "You're not really thinking about jumping in there, are you?"

"Maybe," said Lewis. ". . . Smells like food in there."

"They have a raw sewage problem out here," the angel explained. "That's not really food. Well, it is in a way, but it's too disgusting to talk about. Even to you. Besides, it's *freezing* in there. Not only will you get hepatitis and a host of other dreadful diseases, the tide will pull you out to sea. The undertow will push you down and hold you under."

"Yes," said Lewis, "but it smells like food in there." He poised once again for the jump.

"Wait. Wait. Lewis. Wait. Or maybe I should phrase it this way: *Stay.* Before you jump and endanger your life in the name of a poisonous hors d'oeuvre, why not stop and consider what life would be like if you had never been born?"

"Huh? What do you mean?"

"Imagine," said the angel, "a world into which you had never been born. Let's look in on Merrill. Your mother. Can you see her? Look."

"Yes," said Lewis, suddenly seeing. "There she is. But what's that she's wearing?"

"On her head? Ah, a hat."

"She never wears a hat," said Lewis.

"No," said the angel, "not since you ate them all. But since you were never born, she has a fine assortment of hats. Look. She's taking that one off and putting on another one."

"My God," said Lewis, feeling little globs of drool beginning to form in the corners of his mouth, "and look what she's got on her feet!"

"Yes," said the angel, "those are the suede boots you ate the day she brought you home from the pound. She has several pairs now. In different styles and colors. To match her hats. And the jackets she's not afraid to buy now either."

"The living room looks different," Lewis noticed.

"Yes," said the angel. "More cushions, for one thing. Lots more cushions. The ones you ate, plus a bunch of new ones."

"And what's that in the middle of the room?" Lewis asked.

"That's the antique coffee table she bought with the money she saved on vet bills. Since you were never born, you never got parvo, and she had an extra eighteen hundred dollars. And of course, once again, since she didn't have to worry that you would wreck it, she's really enjoying it. Notice how she gazes at it so fondly. And notice all those fragile little crystal items she has displayed on its surface."

"Geez," said Lewis, "and who the hell is *that*?"

"That's her amazingly well behaved new dog, Phil," said the angel. "She got him out of the pound the same day she didn't get you because you had never been born. He's one of those naturally attentive, obedient, smart dogs who doesn't even require a trainer. Look how he sits at her feet and adores her. People are telling her that he could be the next Benji, or Lassie. She's already had offers from movie companies and dog-food manufacturers who are interested in him for commercials."

"I can't take this," said Lewis. "I have to get over there right away. All that extra income will corrupt her. She really *needs* me."

"Go to her, Lewis," said the angel. "Go to her. Return to her life and remind her that materialism is a superficial value. Teach her to cope with loss. Discourage her from being such a damn control freak. Remember, Lewis . . . no dog's life is a failure so long as he still has expensive items to shred."

And so, the angel watched as the big wet dog galumph-galumph-galumphed back to his home.

Ed Is Coming
to Town!

When love relationships are over, people have different ways of getting on with their lives. Some stay in touch with their exes, redefine the broken bonds, and become friends. Others absorb themselves in acts of violence and spite. And then there are those who put the past behind them and simply get on with the business of living. Let's say, for the sake of argument, that you're mature enough to be one of the latter.

But say the person with whom you have broken up is a public figure. Let's call this old boyfriend of yours "Ed." Maybe both you and Ed worked in media during your relationship so you were used to publicity and fame playing a certain part in the proceedings. Fine. No big deal so far.

But then what if, say, after you broke up, his career began to escalate rather dramatically and he was all over the place with alarming regularity? Still, it didn't have that much effect on you because you moved to the opposite coast and it's pretty easy to avoid scheduled TV appearances. Okay, so maybe more and more you find pictures of Ed making sneak attacks from the newspaper or magazine lying at the base of the Stair-Master you're on. So you see Ed grinning at you almost every time you open your *TV Guide*. Big deal. Don't buy *TV Guide*.

But then say it escalates one step further—to a point where you begin to think that maybe God is writing a new Kafka novel and has decided to give you the lead. What other expla-nation could there be for the fact that suddenly everywhere you drive in your own town you encounter entire billboards featuring a photo of Ed beaming down at you? And not just the occasional billboard, mind you. One on almost every block. And what if, simultaneously, nearly every time you punch the buttons on your car radio to listen to your usual dopey stations, you're caught off-guard by an announcer screaming: "LOOK OUT, EVERYONE! ED IS COMING TO TOWN!" And what if everything culminates in a moment when you find yourself listening to one of those announce-ments while simultaneously looking up at a billboard of Ed?

So let's say you retreat to the sanctuary of your own home to eat some dinner and distract yourself with a little prime-time trash TV. And the first thing you hear from your set is: "Coming up next on *Hard Copy* . . . 'The Girlfriends of Ed!' " Stunned, you sit there and have a little debate with yourself: Should you leave the TV on? As a former girlfriend of Ed's, you can't help but be curious. It's been quite a while since you broke up. Will they mention you? You think they probably won't. But let's say that, against your better judgment, you leave the TV on. And as you sit there in your own home, you feel your jaw dropping when you realize that not only are they *mentioning* you on *Hard Copy,* they have built the entire episode around you. For some reason the reporters were too lazy to get any information about Ed's fifteen million other ex-girlfriends, but managed to find tons of clips that have you in them. Which is when you realize you can't hear what the show is saying about you because the cuckoo-clock noises in your head are drowning out the sound.

But, okay, okay, okay—you compose yourself. You're overreacting. Good thing you have tickets to hear some music that night. Give you a chance to regain some perspective. So let's say you go to a concert—maybe it's someone like Elvis Costello—and about fifteen minutes into the show the performer looks out at the audience and asks: "Hey! Anyone here see Ed last night?" And the whole audience cheers.

What would *you* do?

Come Dine
with Me in 1093

They used to call it the Dark Ages when I was first learning the names of historical periods back in grade school. And that phrase still colors all my associations with the Middle Ages: feudalism, bloodletting and leeches, hooded monks chanting mournfully and flagellating themselves in dank, torch-lit corridors, chastity belts, the Hundred Years War, the Black Plague. And of course the more I dwell on these images, the hungrier I get for a three-course chicken dinner with herb-baked potato and a fruity wine cocktail. Which is why I am very lucky that one of the Medieval Times Dinner and Tournament Restaurant franchises ("where the year is 1093 A.D. and you are the guests of the royal castle") is only about a two-hour drive from my house. Talk about the promise of a rousing good time! Pinch me! I must be dreaming!

I probably would have gone there sooner, but until last week I could never get any of my so-called friends to say yes to an invitation to join me . . . even after I offered to pay! And it didn't really sound like the kind of place I could go to by myself and sit inconspicuously in a corner, pretending to be lost in important thought. So I was both impressed and grateful when my friends Polly and Michael not only didn't back out on me at the last minute but also didn't bolt out of the car as we turned into the parking lot of the only castle on the block.

"I didn't realize that the parking in the Middle Ages was this bad," Michael whines as he nervously comprehends for the first time what exactly he is going to be expected to put up with.

I myself begin to get swept up in the spirit of the Middle Ages (or maybe I just begin to feel middle-aged) pretty much from the moment I purchase our tickets next to the life-size mural of the caped and armored knights of the realm, right beneath the giant sign welcoming all patrons to "Visit our museum of torture." Apparently back in 1093 that was what they did with their evenings instead of watching sitcoms.

Moments later Michael comes bounding back from the room labeled LORDS to report, "I hear a toilet flushing and a dude wearing a tunic and tights comes out and washes his hands."

"There was a woman in a long green gown with a veil and gloves in the next stall in the ladies' room," says Polly. So now we know for sure we're not in Kansas anymore. Although, who knows—Medieval Times is a chain. There *may* be one just like this in Kansas.

Anyway, first thing on the agenda is to partake of the medieval tradition of being photographed with an old bearded guy in a cape and a crown. No one seems to know who he is. We all keep our fingers crossed that he is not armed and does in fact have a job here. A quote in my orientation brochure reads, "My noble guests, you honor me with your presence. I, Don Raimundo II, Count of Perelada, welcome you to my castle for an evening of sumptuous feasting and spectacular pageantry." I have a feeling this may be Don. And how interesting to note that in the ensuing nine hundred years the phrase "you honor me with your presence" has been changed to mean "You must pay me thirty dollars if you want to come in."

"Working here is just like being back in high school again," the "ticket wench" tells me after I finish having my picture taken. "The knights are the jocks. The managers are the principals. The tech crew are the druggies." I always suspected the Crusades were just a big pep rally. But before I even get to find out who the bartenders are, a couple of men in velveteen tunics carrying horns (the pep band?) step onto a little stage to call for our attention with a brief but alarming duet. "What do you call that kind of music?" I ask Michael, because he is a professional musician and I am an eager student of history. "I call that some sad shit," he replies.

Now a guy with a manicured beard wearing a robe and a cape comes forward to make some kind of proclamation. He is speaking with the kind of generic Shakespearean accent that could get him work selling mutton at a Renaissance Faire. His message elicits such a wildly enthusiastic response from the crowd that I cannot hear what he has said. "Sorry, I didn't catch it either," the cheering guy beside me explains, not letting that dampen his enthusiasm. But no matter, because now it is time to take our seats at tables that surround a large exhibition ring. We are all wearing colored paper crowns that correspond both to the tablecloth colors and to the teams of knights for whom we are expected to cheer. Those of us who are attending unaccompanied by children under the age of ten are hoping we look like very good sports and not complete idiots.

"Hi. I'm Rick, your slave and manservant," says a guy in an

apron and two different colors of pant legs. "M'lady, may I present your dinner?" Of course! Dinner presentation! Always a welcome part of the medieval dining-out experience. And so I have placed before me a small plate of middle-aged celery and a large silver cauldron of some kind of reddish canned soup. Simultaneously the air is filled with more staccato horn bursts ("Something from *Fiddler on the Roof,* I think," says Michael) and out into the ring rides a gorgeous young man upon a valiant steed. (Or maybe it was the other way around.) "The cute one with the really long hair is my boyfriend," whispers the "beverage wench" to me. I think she means the *guy.* "He works with L.A. Models. Care for another fruity wine cocktail this evening?" In the high school that is Medieval Times, she is a cheerleader. Manservant Rick is a shop teacher.

"Does the soup not please m'lady?" he nails me, paying what I am starting to feel is entirely *too much* attention to my eating habits. "No, no, it's fine," I lie. "I just have a little touch of the bubonic plague. But I think it's just the twenty-four-hour kind."

And now into the show ring a dark-hooded, hunchbacked monk appears in a cloud of smoke. There is a weird foreboding music and chanting that I can't quite make out. "Who *is* that?" I ask my manservant Rick. "I'm sorry," he replies, "I really can't tell you. I've only been working here about three weeks." "I used to know but I forgot," says the beverage wench. "I can go in the back and check for you. Anyone care for another fruity wine cocktail?"

"Let's move on to happier matters," says the emcee as the spooky monk suddenly takes a powder. "My lords and ladies! A toast! To the knights of the realm!" Everyone cheers as Don Raimunda drinks an entire goblet of something. I'm not sure why this gets cheers. Perhaps just to celebrate the fact that a guy his age gets paid to wear a crown and drink a beverage for a living. Pretty good gig!

"M'lady is not hungry tonight?" says manservant Rick, on my case again. "Are you not feasting well tonight?" He is starting to give me the willies. "Yes, yes, I'm feasting perfectly well tonight," I snap at him. Feeling guilty, I try to talk to him honestly. Turns out manservant Rick used to be a contractor who fell on hard times. "Ten ninety-three was a bad year for home improvement," says Michael.

Now all around us the cheering has grown intense as the knights on horseback in the arena knock themselves and each other out jousting and running relays. "The one in the red cape is also a professional surfer," the beverage wench tells me. "He just got engaged. Are you going to want to purchase any photos this evening?" Now she has the *nerve* to try to sell us mounted photos of a bunch of bleary-eyed jerks wearing paper crowns and drinking from goblets. Ha-ha-ha. They think they're so damn funny. Whoops! Those are pictures of us.

"We welcome here tonight fifty-eight strong from the Kingdom of Shell Oil," booms our emcee. "Also, Jeffrey and Kimberly announce their engagement." I look over at my friend Michael. His crown is falling down across his nose as he slides into his "pastries of the castle." He has fallen asleep. It is now the unanimous opinion of the lords and ladies at our table that it's time to head back to the future, which looks a good deal more attractive than it did a few hours ago.

On the drive home we try to evaluate the lessons of history we have learned.

"It *was* just like the 1100s," says Michael. "The 1100 block of Broadway."

As for me, I am deeply relieved to be returning to a time when no one constantly monitors my food intake and calls me m'lady.

They say that those who do not learn from history are doomed to repeat it. So I would like to think that I learned as much as I was meant to because I really don't care to go through all of that again anytime soon.

If I Could Talk to the Animals

I have four dogs. This makes me a woman who lives in a herd. Naturally I talk to my dogs all day long. But although these conversations are frequent, they are admittedly kind of light on content. The most commonly spoken exchange is a version of "Okay, so *now* what?"

Like many pet lovers, I have often dreamed of one day being able to *really* talk with my dogs, despite the fact that I know I would not want to hear a lot of what they have to say. Topics such as sex, parasites, and butt itch would be better left uncommented upon.

But if I could talk to my dogs, I would dearly love to get some explanations. For instance, why, when I walk in the door, does my dog Bo run to get a stuffed animal and then disappear under the dining room table? For self-esteem reasons, I've chosen to interpret this behavior as "overwhelmed by delight," rather than "overcome with terror." Like so much of what my dogs do, it makes no literal sense. That is why I have come to think of my dogs as exchange students from another planet where there are few, if any, academic requirements.

I was harboring no illusions about a deeper kind of "interspecies communication" until recently, when I learned about a larger-than-you-might-imagine group of people all over this great land of ours who call themselves "interspecies communicators." Members of this group claim that they are able to hold the kind of conversations with animals that many of us are not even able to hold with other people unless we are in a really, really good mood. Not only do these "interspecies communicators" say they can experience two-way verbal exchanges with the house pet of your choice, but they offer their services for sale in a counseling capacity.

These people live in a version of the world I have wanted to believe exists since I read my first fairy tale. It is that children's-book world of magical powers, in which you get to warn a herd of deer that hunting season is about to begin and then have them turn up to thank you, the way they did for Dawn Heyman, a communicator who is booked up for weeks in advance.

Who would pay money for such a service? Well, I am their perfect client. So I decided to contact a number of interspecies communicators to see what I could learn.

Before we began, I decided to lay down a few ground rules for myself in order to evaluate the authenticity of the experience. Since my goal was to be convinced that an actual two-sided animal-to-human conversation had taken place I decided that the unanswered background questions I have about my dog Winky, whom I found loose on Pacific Coast Highway, would provide a way to measure the truth. If any of these animal communicators was actually talking to Winky, there would be some consistency in the details of their stories.

Communication Attempt Number 1

Available the same night I called her was "Marcia," a retired teacher in her sixties who one day heard animals talking to her as though she "was channeling them." Her ad for "psychic communication with your pets" was running in the "Counseling, Education and Spiritual Resources" section of one of those free Los Angeles New Age publications that sit in giant piles on the floors of coffeehouses and gyms.

"Cats will carry on a conversation with you like you won't believe," she tells me, when I call to make an appointment. She recalls that the talkiest animal she ever met was a six-month-old guinea pig who had a feeling that she was supposed to mate but wasn't sure what was expected of her. Luckily, Marcia knew enough about the details of guinea pig dating to be able to offer helpful advice.

"Dogs do speak and understand English," she tells me, as I look around the room at an immense amount of circumstantial evidence to the contrary. To converse with my dogs, Marcia will speak to them all on the phone. None of my dogs gets many phone calls, so this is shaping up as a special occasion.

That evening at the appointed time I called Marcia's number. She suggested we begin by asking my dogs who wanted to go first. I did, but no one looked up from licking their body parts. Not wanting to hurt Marcia's feelings, I assigned the task to my biggest dog, Lewis.

"Hold the phone up to his head," said Marcia. This could only be accomplished by hanging on to his collar to keep him from running out of the room. While I restrained him, I could hear Marcia cooing soothingly through the receiver, seemingly unaware that the expression on Lewis's usually friendly face indicated he thought the telephone was a torture device by which he was going to meet a painful death.

"You're a big boy, aren't you," I heard her say to him, repeating the information I had given her. "How do you like being a big boy?" ("Do you know what he said to me?" she asked me later, chuckling. "He said, 'It gets me around.' He has a very laid-back sense of humor.")

As soon as his part of the phone call was finished, Lewis put his tail between his legs and ran into the backyard. Marcia now picked up the conversation with my smallest dog, Winky. "He said he likes music, especially slow waltzes," she reported, making me wonder where he had come into contact with waltzes of any speed. But since he seemed in the mood to talk, I asked her to find out why he was loose on the highway the day I found him.

"He told me that the maid on a big estate left the back door open," she said. "Apparently he wandered off and couldn't find his way back."

Certainly a plausible enough story, were it not for the fact that he said something different to Dawn Heyman.

Communication Attempt Number 2

I had my phone appointment with thirty-four-year-old Dawn Heyman a couple of weeks later. A former social worker, Dawn was the founder of Spring Farm Cares, a farm-animal sanctuary in Clinton, New York. "It's the world's first center for the teaching of interspecies communication, serving fifty states, Canada, Europe, Saudi Arabia, and Australia," she tells me. She then mentions, offhandedly, that one of the buildings at Spring Farm was designed by one of her cats. Okay, yes, this sounds kind of absurd on the face of it, until you take into account that the cat in question was an architect in a past life. When I display a little skepticism, Dawn is completely unfazed. She is used to a bad attitude from laypeople. That is why she always explains to her workshop students that the early stages of communicating with animals can feel like "you are just making it all up. If you can imagine what your dog is saying, nine times out of ten that *is* what he is saying," she goes on. The proof she offers is the way in which so many people at workshops end up having the same exact anecdotal exchange with a particular goat or sheep. This explains why they're so seldom invited to dinner parties.

Which is not to say that animal content is not sometimes unpredictable. There was the time Dawn's horse confided that she was "really upset about what was going on in the Mideast." When Dawn inquired how the horse knew about the Mideast, she learned that the birds had been leaking the details. "Birds are the news gatherers of the animal world," she tells me. (Although I heard from one of my dogs that a lot of birds are just getting their info from reading the papers at the bottom of their cages.)

Now it was time to talk to my dogs. But unlike Marcia, Dawn didn't have me hold the phone up to anyone's head. In fact, it was fine with Dawn that all four of her subjects were fast asleep on the floor. When I asked if I should wake them, she said I needn't bother.

We began with Tex, my problem dog, who was rescued

from a homeless guy. Tex was suffering from such bad separation anxiety that when I left the house, he ate through door frames and parts of the wall. "He feels a lot of fear because he lived in other homes where, as soon as he relaxed and felt happy, they got rid of him," Dawn tells me. "He needs to know his role in your home. He wants to know what he can do to help you." Toward this end, she gave him an exercise that she felt was going to help relax him. She told him that when I left the house, it was his job to make sure everything stayed exactly the same.

This sounded like a great plan, and it worked very well until Tex ate my bathroom windowsill later that week.

Which brought us to Winky, who was under the table, on his back, snoring loudly.

"He talks really fast," she said. "He says he feels good. He's really happy. He likes to eat and he likes his toys."

"What does he tell you about his past?" I asked her.

"He says he lived in a very nice home with children and another dog. And he was very happy. Until one day he began following another dog around a supermarket parking lot. He got lost and couldn't find his way back to the car."

Certainly a plausible story. Just not the story the little psycho told Gerri Ryan less than twenty-four hours later.

Communication Attempt Number 3

Gerri Ryan has a Ph.D. in clinical psychology and used to counsel couples until she "underwent a change in spiritual outlook" and began to have more profound relationships with her companion animals. Her credentials in interspecies discussion were many and varied. Not only had she counseled horses about postpartum depression, she once convinced the bacteria infecting a llama to vacate the premises so the llama could heal. But the bacteria had to survive and make babies, they told her. Which is when it occurred to her to tell those single-celled narcissists that there was a manure pile in the back of the house. As it turned out, this was just the change of scenery the bacteria needed. Two days later, both llama and bacteria were healthy and happy and living apart.

Like Dawn Heyman, Gerri Ryan had more work than she could handle. Our appointment was delayed because she was talking to each of fourteen unsettled cats belonging to a couple who were moving to a new house. The cats were clearly un-nerved by this, suddenly peeing everywhere. Gerri was trying to work things out with them, one cat at a time.

It seemed almost anticlimactic to ask her to chat with Winky. But she agreed, and her methodology was her own. After asking for a physical description, she disappeared for fif-teen minutes while I hung around waiting on the phone. When she returned, she had already talked with Winky at length. He told her about a green chew toy that was his special favorite. Although Winky is a boy who has many toys, includ-ing a number of stuffed animals with whom he has sex every morning after breakfast, if there was a green chew toy in his life, I had yet to meet it.

Moving on to his past, Winky was very forthcoming for the third time. But this time he claimed he was driving at night with a well-built, jovial man wearing coveralls. Appar-ently this guy pulled the car into a park out in the country and left Winky behind. He drove off and abandoned him. Natu-rally, Winky had "lots of hurts from this for a very long time.

But now he had said his good-byes and made peace. He no longer misses them."

Conclusions

So after two weeks of sitting by patiently while my dogs hogged the phone, I came to the following conclusions: The animal communicators with whom I spoke all seemed like nice, sincere people. They seemed to genuinely love animals and believe that their work was for real.

But judging by the three-pronged saga of Winky's mysterious past, either some of these people are delusional or my dog Winky is a sociopath.

Cell Phone Etiquette

I know I am not the only person who is growing increasingly irritated with the way my fellow Americans have become obsessed en masse with talking on cell phones. Ever since cell phones caught on in such a behemoth way, everyone is suddenly under the impression that they need to be on the phone *all the time.*

Pre–cell phone, I don't remember seeing people lined up by the hundreds on street corners, in the parking lots of gas stations, and in front of supermarkets waiting for a chance to use the pay phones. In fact, believe it or not, people used to spend a portion of the day totally and completely phoneless!

Now these very same people seem to think they cannot really go anywhere or do anything at all unaccompanied by a phone. They feel a true sense of deprivation if they cannot make phone calls on the land, on the sea, and in the air. And with the rise of this obsessive-compulsive need for continuous phoning, phone decorum, along with any respect for the privacy of others, has melted away like the snows of yesteryear.

Not very long ago, being in a commercial establishment constituted a shared experience among a random assortment of like-minded patrons. *Here we are all here in this drafty hallway/annoyingly crowded airport lounge/ridiculously loud, poorly lit Afro-French bistro,* we would silently think, as a group. *Like it or not, we are all in this together.*

Now, because of the intrusive and domineering nature of cell phone yakkers who blithely force us to listen to private musings meant for the ears of someone we cannot even see, we find ourselves unwillingly preoccupied by the dopey details of some stranger's dinner plans, business dealings, or marital woes, all of which we know are none of our business. They force us into a position of feeling like nosy, snooping interlopers even though we are every bit as entitled as they to be wherever we are—wasting our hard-earned money on overpriced coffee concoctions or violent, ill-conceived, poorly plotted summer movie blockbusters.

A couple of weeks ago I read an editorial in *The New York Times* by a writer named Sharon White Taylor in which she made a plea for someone to develop some hard-and-fast cell phone etiquette.

I have risen to the challenge. Please regard the following as a sancrosact edict, not unlike an amendment to the Constitution.

Cell Phone Etiquette— Defy It at Your Own Risk!!!

As it is impolite to place cell phone calls at a distance of *less than* fifteen *feet* from another person, we hold these truths to be self-evident:

A. The interior of a commercial establishment is to be regarded as an *equally shared airspace,* not to be vocally dominated by one person more than another. Which is why it follows that the situations listed hereunder are inappropriate for placing, receiving, or otherwise engaging in any and all cell phone calls:

1. At the Table in a Restaurant

It is impolite to place or to receive a cell phone call when in the presence of dining companions. Group dining was developed as a ritual of camaraderie and communion among those *at the table only.*

It is also impolite for the waiter or waitress to place or receive phone calls while taking an order or bringing the food. If the chef in the kitchen is back there talking on his cell phone while he is making something with balsamic vinegar, this is permissible as long as he is not visible to the dining population.

2. At a Theatrical Event

It is definitely *not* okay for audience members to place or receive phone calls in or around any kind of theatrical venue. So, too, is it inappropriate for the performers on the stage or in the orchestra pit. A good rule of thumb is this: If you have a program in your hand, or are already dressed in your Elizabethan costume, turn your cell phone off and put it away.

This rule also extends to the placing or receiving of cell phone calls during a movie. Even a very, very bad movie. With the possible exception of an Adam Sandler movie, when it is permissible to receive a maximum of two calls from licensed health care professionals, concerned about your mental state and trying to talk you out of there.

3. Inside a Lavatory Stall

The presence of unseen strangers, even those only present via cell phone, is not welcome among the pantsless during the vulnerable *Homo sapiens* waste elimination process.

4. In the Supermarket

This also includes the pharmacy, the hardware store, and any storelike place in a mall. The other day I found myself shopping for groceries next to a guy on a cell phone who was selecting his purchases, one at a time, via a tedious discussion with God only knows who. I can only hope the person on the other end of the phone had the sense to break up with him later that evening. He does not deserve to have a happy home life.

5. In the Elevator

Allow us to share our precious between-floor-transit moments together in complete silence.

6. While Dancing, or During Any Activity That Involves an Embrace

This, of course, implies *no cell phoning during sex*. With the *one* exception of any sexual situation in which a partner has refused to perform any sort of foreplay, but then proceeds to whale away for a really long time regardless. Under these circumstances, it is okay to place calls to taped messages such as Moviephone or 900-number horoscopes which involve only listening, but not talking.

7. At the Doctor's Office

When in the examining room, it is not appropriate for the physician, dentist, surgeon, attending nurse, or patient to place or receive personal cell phone calls during any tedious, nerve-racking, or potentially humiliating medical treatment.

B. *Don't forget the great outdoors.* This includes *anywhere* in, on, or around water, such as poolside situations, snorkeling, deep-sea diving, hot-tubbing, waterskiing, and boating. It is also impolite to take or receive phone calls in the bathtub or on the toilet. (See also #3.)

Likewise *the wilderness.* Cell phones are not to be taken on nature hikes, to national parks, or on rock-climbing expeditions. No one came all that way, not to mention spent all that money on the special shoes, just to listen to someone else's phone conversation.

Well, there is much more to be said. But I don't want to risk requiring too much of a hostile and unruly public all at once. Kindly memorize the above. When it is fully integrated into society as we know it, I will let you know what I expect from you next.

My Career
in Stun Guns

I live in Los Angeles because I am a frequent employee of what we refer to as the entertainment industry. And one of the by-products of that liaison is being "invited" to join an awful lot of labor unions. Which is why I've been a dues-paying member of the Writers Guild of America for about ten years, although I'd managed to avoid any gathering of more than three writers in one place at one time until last week, when I decided to go down to the Hollywood Palladium and see if I could find out why, as a member of the Writers Guild, I had been on strike for four months. This being my first-ever union meeting, I can offer no comparisons, except that I think there are probably fewer pudgy minoxidil users in rimless glasses and sleeveless sweater vests in attendance at a giant meeting of the International Brotherhood of Teamsters.

As for the content of the meeting, it fluctuated wildly between a very dull point-by-point reading of the proposed contract and some extremely raucous shouting, complete with the wild hissing, booing, and cheering one might expect at one of

Saddam Hussein's rallies. There were no refreshments and no fabulous door prizes, and no one besides me was interested in doing "the wave."

Yet, while I had gone into the meeting unfocused, alienated, and kind of irritated, I left feeling rather impressed by the passion that members seemed to have for continuing the strike. And in trying to cope with the idea of *even more* striking, I became aware that the reason I'd tended to avoid previous Writers Guild meetings was my growing disenchantment with the field of TV scriptwriting. So maybe my whole forced retirement was just a sign from God that it was time to select a more suitable career. Which is why I got up the next morning and started carefully reading the help-wanted ads, searching for beacons that might light the way to a brighter tomorrow.

1. Selling Stun Guns: A Career Just for Me?

No wonder I got excited. The ad said, "Make big money selling the revolutionary stun gun," and what little girl doesn't grow up hoping to hear herself one day speak the words "Any stun guns for you today, sir or ma'am?" Of course my heart was racing with anticipation as I dialed the number. A woman answered and told me someone would call me back. I didn't realize how unnerved I was by this until I heard myself tell her that my name was Monica. When the phone rang just a few minutes later, I jumped. A man's voice said, "Hello, Monica?" and I felt the blood drain from my head. Just yesterday I had been a slightly respected member of the community, and now strange men were phoning me at home and calling me Monica. "What's all that clicking on the line?" the guy asked. "I don't like all that clicking. I better call you back." He hung up, and I briefly considered not answering when he called back. Maybe weapon sales wasn't the ideal career for me. "How about if I just come down to your headquarters?" is what I eventually said to the guy. "We don't have a headquarters," he told me, but he would "arrange to meet anywhere you'd like. We're a fly-by-night organization." "So I guess that means you don't have a medical or dental plan" is what I said, but I was thinking, *Boy! This is too good to be true! An opportunity to go to an undisclosed location and meet a strange man from a fly-by-night organization who is driving around with a trunk full of weapons! Pinch me! I must be dreaming!* "I'm going to have to think about it" is what I eventually replied as I reopened the want ads.

2. Stun Guns Part Two: The Adventure Continues

"Sell Stun Guns! Promote Peace! Prevent Violence! Make Quick Cash Daily!" said the ad right under the first ad. Now *here* was an attractive package—international diplomacy and high-stakes capitalism neatly rolled into one. Okay, I'd been burned before, but by now I kind of liked the idea of telling people that I was professionally "into stun guns." It had a crisp, dignified ring to it. So I dialed this number with a lot more enthusiasm and confidence—or at least that's what I thought I was doing until I heard myself tell the salesman who answered the phone that my name was Monica. "You have a nice voice, Monica," the guy on the phone said. "I'll bet you could sell stun guns." Suddenly I felt the room spinning and my skin growing damp and clammy—the combination of a goofy alias and a violent weapon being used in the same sentence was making me swoon. But on the bright side, this guy *did* have a headquarters, and so I found myself walking up to the door of a small white stuccoed house on a busy street, across from a retirement home and directly next door to COMPLETE BRIDAL SERVICE, EVERYTHING FOR THE WEDDING (which I figured probably was a prime location for this kind of business, considering the potential for shared referrals).

Outside the front door was a large, colorful lottery wheel, and beneath it was a crude painting of a rainbow with a pot of gold at the end. A man of about forty-five, sporting the always-fashionable Harpo Marx hairstyle, opened the door and invited me into a small but tidy living room. "Why are you looking around all nervous?" he said. "We're a licensed lottery dealer. That ought to make you feel safer." And of course once I realized that, I relaxed immediately—cushioned by the knowledge that lottery dealers are the moral backbone of every community. "Have you ever seen a stun gun?" he asked, instructing me to sit down on a sad old couch directly across from a large pyramid-style display of various hair-care products: shampoo, creme rinse, styling gel, mousse, extra-body conditioner . . . a perfect addition to the decor of any smart room.

"Do you know what a stun gun is?" he asked, disappearing into a back room. "No," I loudly confessed, "I barely know what a creme rinse is." He returned and sat down uncomfortably close to me on the couch, removing from a box another black box about the size of a cassette player. "*This* is a stun gun," he told me. "When you push the trigger here, it sends out a jolt of electricity. It's forty-five thousand volts. It's the only legal self-defense weapon that you can carry concealed." He held the thing out in front of my face and squeezed the trigger, causing a bright blue miniature lightning bolt to jump from one point to another and causing me to jump from one point to another as well. "The way it works is we sell them to you by the dozen for $30 apiece, and then you resell them for $79.95 . . . but to tell you the truth, your personality . . . the way you react to the guns . . . ," he said, hesitating, "well, it's obvious you're uncomfortable with them, and if *you* don't like them you're not going to have a lot of luck selling them." Somehow I knew there was a grain of truth in this. So I knocked him down and, grabbing the stun gun, zapped him. Then, when he was out for the count, I shampooed and moussed up his hair. (Okay, I made that last part up, but, as may be clear by now, I left there still thinking like a writer. I knew I hadn't found my new career yet.)

3. Ad Number Three: My Career as a Professional Hypnotist

"Earn while you learn," the ad said. "No college education required." And while it was too late to do anything about erasing the latter, the idea of having my own little club act where I could wear a gown and humiliate audience volunteers had me nearly paralyzed with joy. Which is why I found myself in a room full of Naugahyde chairs in a building just a few doors down from the Hot Legs Boutique in midtown Van Nuys. We were a small group and so ill at ease that none of us could even look at one another, so we were relieved when a thirtyish man with a mustache (who looked like the "after" photo in a men's styling salon) came in and dimmed the lights. He instructed us to watch the TV monitor at the front of the room.

"We are going to learn all about Marlo Thomas's unusual new movie with Kris Kristofferson," an announcer's voice boomed as we watched the opening credits for *PM Magazine.* "Plus, we'll find out about a *miraculous cure for everything*!" Right away I suspected that *one* of these two probably had something to do with hypnosis. And sure enough, seconds later we dropped Marlo like a hot potato and met Carol, a singer who was plagued by some kind of mysterious vocal obstruction until she turned to hypnosis, at which time, she said, she "discovered my own knowingness." Seconds later, Florence Henderson was seen chatting with Merv Griffin about how hypnosis allowed *her* to "go back in and clean out the areas of your life that bother you." (By this I assumed she meant that whole unfortunate Wessonality campaign, unless she meant those endless reruns of *The Brady Bunch*.)

When the segment was over, the guy from the styling salon photo rejoined our group. "What kind of people did you just see using hypnosis?" he asked us. "Were they reasonable people? Functional people? Normal people with normal problems?" No one said anything right away, maybe because we all had the feeling that the jury was still out on Florence Henderson. So to loosen us up a bit he had us go around the room and introduce ourselves. The girl with the fluffy hair was a receptionist at a local TV station. The white-haired guy next to her was unemployed. The hip-looking guy next to him was in music publishing and used to manage big moneymaking bands in the sixties. And the oily-haired guy soaking in cheap cologne to my left was a security guard. As for me, I was just a happy little woman named Monica who had a dream of a nightclub career where I could take audience volunteers and stretch them out stiff as a board between two chairs.

With some annoyance the instructor informed me that this was not *that* kind of hypnosis. This was for midcareer people who want to work in a "therapy-related field" but don't want to spend eight to ten years getting a psychology credential. The twenty-four-hour beginning class ($295) would enable students to begin to see clients professionally *in just twelve weeks*. And by the end of the first year's internship here a trainee hypnotist could figure on making $20,000 to $50,000. As I looked over the application forms, I had to admit I felt spooked by the notion that in less than three months some civilian who wanted to stop smoking or who was experiencing stress might find him- or herself growing sleepy by gazing into the eyes of a security guard.

"Anyone can print up a sign and just *say* they're a hypnotist," said our instructor, "but *we* are approved by the State Superintendent of Public Instruction." I thought about that and, deciding that the first way was more to my liking, headed out the door to check out the cost of printing up a sign. I had mixed feelings—sadness, because I hadn't found my new career, and happiness, because the strike had given me the free time to check out some very important new options. "Train to be a model, or just look like one," said the next ad on the page. Now *here* was a career that just maybe I could be comfortable with. I wonder what they pay you to just look like a model?

Firing My Dog

The recession is something that affects each American differently. But as I sat staring it in the face, it occurred to me that there were some obvious ways to cut my expenses dramatically. Which is why, one day in late summer, I called for my new dog Lewis to come into my office. Since he never comes when I call him, I finally gave up and succeeded in locating him out in the yard underneath a hedge, where I was able to make him stop digging and look me in the eye.

Me: Lewis . . .

Lewis: Help me pull these impatiens out of the ground.

Me: No. Stop that. Leave those shrubs alone.

Lewis: Just take part of this in your mouth and pull on it. I think it is almost loose enough to uproot.

Me: No! Stop it! No! This is exactly what I wanted to talk to you about. I realize you're just out of puppyhood and all, but you are very destructive, very poorly behaved, and you are costing me an incredible amount of money.

Lewis: Well, this has been fascinating but sorry, I can't stay. You don't expect me to sit here and destroy just this one plant all afternoon.

Me: Lewis. Listen to me. I've been going through my financial records and it comes to my attention that I've been spending several hundred dollars per month on you, minimum. And to be frank, I'm having a great deal of difficulty justifying that kind of financial outlay.

Lewis: Cost-of-living increases. Services rendered. Do I have to itemize them for you?

Me: Services rendered? Yes, do that. Go ahead and itemize them for me. *What services rendered?*

Lewis: Well, for example, shrub removal runs you eight bucks an hour. It's demanding work.

Me: You mean you're *charging* me for ruining my yard? I already pay a bunch of guys from El Salvador to do that.

Lewis: They're not thorough. I gotta move. Come with me. It'll save you money. You know, sitting here at your feet goes for six bucks an hour.

Me: Am I hearing correctly? You charge me to sit at my feet?

Lewis: Of course I charge you. You see anyone else sitting at your feet voluntarily?

Me: I'm stunned. What else do you charge for?

Lewis: Room-to-room barking. You don't get a service like that for nothing. Ball's got a ten-buck-an-hour one-hour minimum.

Me: I can't get over this. You *charge* me to play ball? I thought you *liked* ball.

Lewis: Guess again. And it's seventy-five bucks an hour to sleep on the bed with you.

Me: Are you serious? You mean I am *paying* you to cover my bed with grime and bugs and hair? What *are* those little hard chunks anyway?

Lewis: Don't worry about those. I throw those in at cost.

Me: You know something, I am *glad* we had this little talk because these are all services I can live without. Plus, you destroy my books. You eat my hats and my shoes. You broke into my closet and ate my souvenir collection.

Lewis: I'm sure there was a work order issued on that. I went into golden time that day. It's dangerous to eat souvenirs. God only knows what they're made of.

Me: Well, that's the last straw. I've heard enough. I'm going to have to let you go. You're fired.

Lewis: You can't just fire me. I have a contract.

Me: Get out.

Lewis: You're looking at a lawsuit, lady.

Me: Fine. Sue me. Get out.

Lewis: I'm not going anywhere. Go ahead. Try and move me. Did you ever try to lift a six-hundred-pound sack of lawn clippings? You aren't going to be able to budge me. I've seen you struggling with the bottled-water refills. And even if you do get me out the front door, I'm just going to stand there and whine and bark ceaselessly until all your neighbors get pissed off at you. Believe me, I'm going *nowhere*. In fact, unless you want to apologize, I might start the barking right now. . . .

Me: No, no. Wait. Don't start barking. . . .

Lewis: Here I go. I don't hear an apology.

Me: Wait, wait. You're on probation. Okay, okay . . . I'm sorry.

Lewis: By the way, "no barking" is three bucks a minute.

A World
Without Men

A couple of weeks ago I attended an inventors' convention at the Pasadena Center Exhibition Building, a large hall
crammed with exhibitors' booths, in which the proud mothers
of new inventions were showing off their bright ideas. What
struck me about the affair was that the overwhelming majority
of these mothers were men.

The inventions were addressed to a wide range of human-
ity's needs, but one of the most popular categories turned out
to be (for reasons I still haven't got a bead on, unless it con-
nects somehow to Jonathan Swift's observation that "man is at
his most contemplative when he is at stool") variations on the
toilet. There were two types of "odorless" toilets, one involving
filters and one involving vacuums and air fresheners. There
was a portable traveler's toilet, a "multi-user entertainment
system super top" toilet, and a toilet-seat alarm system that
was activated whenever anyone forgot to put the seat back
down. And even *that* was invented by a man.

Another man, named Sergio Regalado, was at the convention trying to mass-market an idea that he claimed was popular in the eighteenth and nineteenth centuries: the tongue scraper. "If you never scrape your tongue, you'll always have bad breath," he vigorously explained, causing a thoughtful listener to shudder at the thought of a minimum of three decades' worth of horrible breath she'd been causing loved ones to endure. Perhaps the goofiest new take on the whole better-health thing came from a scientist and engineer called Dr. Edward Richards, who, in addition to having invented some canoe-shaped, wheel-laden airplane-landing-gear deal, had also brought along the plans and prototypes for the "medical muffler device," which, says the press release, "allows gas from the gastrointestinal tract to escape slowly, silently, continually and odorless." "My grandchild had a problem with the gas release," he explained to me in a deadly somber Slavic accent of some kind, "and it was hell for everyone." And thus was born an invention.

On the drive home I found myself wondering why it was that so few women had seen fit to contribute to an event such as this. To be fair, there *had* been a couple. Offhand, I could think of two I had seen. Both had invented new types of dolls. This, as compared with one wild-eyed man who had bothered to reinvent the alphabet and intended to try to push it forward until every single piece of printed material in the world had been redone to his specifications. The explanation I came up with for the paucity of female crackpot inventors was that they probably had something better to do. Women just didn't want to bother inventing a toilet-seat alarm when they already had devices such as yelling, pouting, and brooding resentfully in pretty good working order. As for the grandchild's problem with the gas release, I don't think a woman would have felt the need for a peculiar plastic muffler deal if she knew about the bran muffin.

As I continued to conjecture along these lines, I began to construct my own crackpot theory with regard to the essential nature of the sexes. My theory is that the very structure of daily life on the planet would have been totally different if there had never been men, since men think so extremely differently from women. To illustrate this, I have compiled a short list of things I feel would never have existed at all had there never been any men.

Mealtimes. Women might have toyed with the idea of sitting down to big plates of several kinds of food three times a day but almost certainly would have rejected it right away because it was so fattening. Instead they would have opted for a few spoons of cottage cheese at 10:30 A.M., an apple at noon, a couple of bites of chocolate-chip cookie at three, forkfuls of whatever someone nearby was eating at around five, and then random nibbling up until bedtime. This syndrome also makes men the rightful heirs to the TV dinner, as I have never met a woman who cared about having a small amount of peas and a tablespoon of mashed potatoes with her Salisbury steak.

Projectile Weaponry. I don't think women would have come up with guns. Maybe not even bows and arrows. In their quest for food, I think, women would have developed concepts along the lines of fly-fishing, wherein one makes little miniatures of the diet of the intended prey to trick it with. But then we might have ended up liking the little miniatures so much that we would keep them for accessories or collectibles, rationalizing that, after all, a handful of grass or berries would be a lot less effort than fish, a lot fewer calories than another plate of greasy ground squirrel.

All Those Different Sports Involving All Those Different Kinds of Balls. Women would have invented one, at most two, really good ones—volleyball and soccer, let's say—and then, figuring that two seemed like plenty, probably would have plowed ahead and developed a multitude of hair-care products. Men, on the other hand, almost definitely would have called it a game after the invention of *one* shampoo, never even bothering to write up the concepts for creme rinses, finishing rinses, or extra-body conditioners, let alone styling gels and mousses.

Various Forms of Entertainment Involving Car Explosions. This category includes TV, movies, races, Grand Prix, and toys that simulate all of the above. I would venture to say that if there had been no men, there almost certainly would not have been any nitro-burning funny cars. In fact, when you consider how enamored women have traditionally been of horses, it makes you wonder if cars would have been invented at all.

Armies. I don't see women dreaming up a highly disciplined, drably outfitted, ordeal-oriented, well-oiled fighting machine. Nah. I also don't think women would have bothered with long-range missile systems—especially after we had worked out all the details of other systems, such as slapping and scratching.

VCRs. Since women have so much trouble operating them, I am going to assume that we wouldn't have bothered with them at all. Though we might have encouraged the invention of TIVO.

All of the above are clear-cut examples of the distinctive approach to logical thought that is unique to men. Of course, this extends into behavior too. Take interior decoration. I don't think the woman has been born to whom it would occur to substitute sports equipment lined up next to the wall for furniture groupings and area rugs. And yet I have frequently visited the "home" of a man who thought this was a fine idea.

It is thought processes like these that eventually find creative release in the invention of tongue scrapers and multiuser entertainment-system toilet-tank tops. Not to mention telephone systems, stereo equipment, and electric carving knives. Those darn men, God bless 'em.

Conversation Piece

I recently spent one of those weeks where I hardly spoke a word out loud. This is the sort of life experience that is almost totally unimaginable in New York City, where one's proximity to complete strangers causes a regular number of pointless verbal exchanges. I call them verbal exchanges because I don't think "I was here first." "Well, what do you want? A medal?" can be classified as a conversation per se.

I have been giving some serious thought to the nature of conversation (as serious as I am capable of) just in case I ever have one again.

First, it is important to note that men and women regard conversation quite differently. For women it is a passion, a sport, an activity even more important to life than eating because it doesn't involve weight gain. The first sign of closeness among women is when they find themselves engaging in endless, secretless rounds of conversation with one another. And as soon as a woman begins to relax and feel comfortable in a relationship with a man, she tries to have that type of conversation with him as well. However, the first sign that a man is feeling close to a woman is when he is comfortable enough to admit that he'd rather she please quiet down so he can hear the TV. A man who feels truly intimate with a woman often reserves for her and her alone the precious gift of one-word answers. Everyone knows that the surest way to spot a successful long-term relationship is to look around a restaurant for the table where no one is talking. Ah . . . now *that's* real love.

But to get to that blissful state, the relationship usually passes through a conversational stage first, which is why I thought I'd take this opportunity to present:

The Merrill Markoe Course in Conversation

What Is a Conversation? For our purposes, it is any exchange of more than two remarks that does not end in an act of violence. The successful conversationalist always remembers to first remove all extraneous objects from the mouth (and hide them, unless you are prepared to make that the topic of the conversation, and quite frankly I have found that admitting "I just *like* the feel of packing materials between my teeth and I don't really care that they're made of toxic chemicals" is not the sort of opening remark that shows one off in the best light).

Always remember to ENUNCIATE clearly. If you notice that the person to whom you are talking is reacting with a blank stare, repeat the phrases "Can you hear me?" and "Do you understand?" in louder and louder tones of voice until you ascertain that your conversational partner (a) does not have a language in common with you, or (b) is in some kind of a stupor. (The former condition is more frequent on the East Coast, the latter on the West. Either situation renders the whole thing pretty hopeless and gives you permission to call a cab.) Which brings us to another basic point: Remember that the creation of new language is the sole domain of advertising copywriters and desperate Scrabble players. And that the words created by these people, such as *Scrumdiddly-umptious, FUNtastic,* and *CHOC-o-licious*—or, in the case of Scrabble, *zziquox*—should never be spoken aloud, even in the privacy of your own home.

Now that we have discussed form, let's move ahead to content.

An important part of any successful conversation is, of course, a good opening remark, one that is designed to intrigue, inspire, and delight. Which is why "Leave me alone," "Please leave me alone," and "Won't you please, please leave me alone" are not good opening remarks. Oddly enough, the opposite—as in "Please, I beg of you, talk to me!"—does not work either. It is considered a turnoff by many. The best opening remark, therefore, is on the surface cheering and neutral but contains an essentially truthful subtext that says, "Do you have the time to listen to me drone on ceaselessly about my problems for as long as I find it convenient?" Examples of this type of opening remark are "Hi. How are you? You look great. That's a very nice purse. Where'd you get it?" and "Hey, what's happening?"

Okay! Now that we've got the old conversational ball rolling, your next important task is to figure out something to say. If you have nothing to say but still feel the need simply to hear yourself talk—maybe just for the facial exercise, or to prove that you're alive—then the appropriate outlet is, of course, talk radio, where a handsomely paid professional moderator is willing to pretend to care about your views on the finalists on *American Idol* or the inflated salaries of professional athletes.

"But," you may say to me, "Merrill, Merrill, Merrill . . . What if I see someone I barely know and want to talk to them? Then what?" And I would say back to you, "First, don't ever use my name three times in a row like that. It puts you well over the legal lifetime limit for using my first name in a sentence." And then I would have to say that this is the best time to use:

The Merrill Markoe Sociological Stereotyping Chart

Clever sociological stereotyping can help you make the sweeping generalizations that are useful conversation starters. Or they will get you a punch in the mouth. Either way you have had that important initial contact with the person of your choice. What I am referring to is the fact that certain types of people are more likely to be interested in certain topics. For example, if you choose "Methods of Scoring Hockey" as your topic of conversation with the average middle-class woman, you're probably making a bad choice. Which is not to say that the average middle-class woman for whom this is a passionate topic does not exist. (Okay. The woman does not exist.) But just as the average middle-class man does not like to talk about his emotions or anything of importance *except* methods of scoring hockey, there is a reason why hockey scoring is the only topic never addressed by Oprah, Dr. Phil, and Regis.

Presented below is a short reference chart indicating some topics and the corresponding demographic sampling that may find them interesting. You will probably want to make up your own list. Or maybe not, if you have any kind of a real life.

Topic	*Who Will Talk About It*
What we as individuals can do to make this planet called Earth a better place to live	Students under the age of twenty-five and sit-com stars who are not getting enough media attention
The plots of highly rated network TV shows such as *Friends* and *Everybody Loves Raymond*	No one. Being forced to listen to this is considered grounds for justifiable homicide in eighteen states
How they score televised sports	Men between the ages of twenty-five and sixty
Why the men in their life won't talk about anything but televised sports	Women between the ages of eighteen and seventy
The weather	Employees of dry-cleaning establishments or the U.S. Postal Service; your parents or, if they're not home, my parents

Topic	*Who Will Talk About It*
The deteriorating health of people you barely know	Your mother or, if she's not home, my mother
What it means that all your man will talk about is sports and all your parents will talk about is the weather and the deteriorating health of people you barely know	Mental health professionals; me

All righty, now that you have successfully initiated the conversation, another problem is likely to present itself. More and more it seems as though a person (and of course by "a person" I mean "me") runs into someone who tells the same story over and over, beat for beat. They never even bother to say "Stop me if you've heard this one before" and do not feel the least bit deterred when they notice that you are mouthing along with them as though you were an audience member at a sing-along. What do you do?

I recommend an exercise that I call creative conversational visualization. As the person drones on, imagine that he is being squashed flat as a bug by a giant steamroller. Now, as you gaze downward at a two-dimensional aerial view of your formerly three-dimensional friend, see if you can answer the following questions: Would he make an interesting piece of abstract art? What sort of frame would you buy for him, and where would you hang it in your home? And, while you're at it, how much do you think you could get for the piece at an art auction? While you proceed with the answers to these questions, do not forget to meet the traditional obligation of "Mmm hmm" and "I see" at five-second intervals.

"But Merrill," you say to me (and of course when I say "you" I mean "me"), "what do I do if I continue to be trapped, a virtual prisoner of dull conversation that threatens to go on until the end of time? Then what?" This is the proper moment for a polite but firm remark that allows you to exit quickly, one that does not hurt the feelings of your conversational partner, such as "I see by my oxygen sensor that there is not enough breathable air on this part of the planet, and since one of us is in danger, I will make the sacrifice and leave." Then you turn on your heel and run like the wind—after, of course, waving a polite good-bye.

Zen and the Art of Multiple Dog Walking

I have four dogs. People say to me, "Four dogs! Why would you have four dogs? Isn't that too many dogs?" and I can only respond, "Yes. It's too many. I don't know why I have four dogs. Now please, please, just leave me alone."

Because I am the kind of person who would *never* give a dog away after I have fallen in love with it (and also the kind of person who falls in love with every dog), I have learned to take a transcendent approach to the challenges presented to me by daily multiple dog management. After all, isn't that the true road to happiness? The ability to meet difficulties and obstacles with grace, energy, and good nature? Which is why I am able to offer:

Zen and the Art of Multiple Dog Walking

It is "walk time." You have put it off as long as possible. But the cyclone of dog activity whirling in the vicinity of the front door indicates that if you put it off much longer you could be eaten alive. So prepare yourself for the walk by focusing on the incredible joy you are bringing to these simple, loving creatures who after all have not nearly as many creative outlets as you do.

As you get the leashes out, repeat this mantra: "I am one with the great joyous spirit that is all men and all beasts." Continue to say this as the dogs hurl themselves at you, knocking you over, making it almost impossible even to hook the leashes to their collars, let alone open the door. Somehow you must let out only two of them, which is the most you have determined you can ever walk safely at one time. Four of them at once is like waterskiing behind the space shuttle.

Having managed this, somehow proceed through the front yard with two fully leashed dogs under control while ignoring the pained, mournful yowls of the two dogs who remain behind, locked in the house. Tell yourself that the neighbors are *not* speculating about what mistreatment you are inflicting on these poor unhappy creatures. They probably can't even hear the ear-piercing shrieks. Certainly they *cannot* be as loud as you imagine.

Jauntily start out down the street, ready now not just to enjoy your "walk" but to appreciate the special way that two entirely different species of warm-blooded mammals can share a single leisure-time pursuit. Hold this thought for as long as possible, particularly when seconds later one of the two dogs wraps himself around a telephone pole and becomes impossible to unwrap because the other dog has continued moving forward in the original trajectory with the same velocity. Do not panic. You will not be ripped in half. Think for a moment about the complex geometry of nature. The way that the earth moves at one orbital speed and the moon and sun at others, while meteors and comets whiz by all over the place and yet there are no collisions. (Well, I suppose there are probably plenty of collisions. But none of them big enough to make the nightly news.)

No, instead they all harmoniously combine to make a perfect solar system, and so it will be with you and the dogs. In just a moment. As soon as you get the one dog untangled. So you call with increasing urgency for the other dog to "STAY!" as you begin to move in the direction in which the leash has wrapped itself around the pole, noticing with amazement how the dog proceeds ahead of you, maintaining a degree of entanglement exactly proportionate to your attempts to unravel him.

Do not grow irritable. Rather, think of the perfection in this movement. Not unlike the perfection of the way water swirls down a drain in one direction on one side of the equator and in another on the other side of the equator. Because so too does the other dog, who weighs 120 pounds, maintain a steady pull in the opposite direction—a pull that seems to be growing ever stronger because he is growling and arching. He is poised momentarily to begin a violent dogfight. The object of his hatred? A completely uninterested dog on the other side of the street who is roaming freely, unencumbered by human supervision. And as this dog gets closer, your dog begins bucking and snarling, baiting him, apparently calling him horrible dog epithets, causing the hair on the neck of the other dog to suddenly stand straight up. Now it becomes apparent that the other dog is in fact a street punk who has probably never lost a fight in his entire life. So you scream at your big fat lardass dog who eats health food and sleeps on your bed to "STAY! I SAID STAY! DON'T YOU MOVE ONE INCH OR I'M GOING TO FIGHT WITH YOU MYSELF!"

And somehow, through the infinite grace of the workings of the universe, for once in your pitiful life he pauses long enough for you to at least unwrap the other leash from around the damn pole. Just in the nick of time, too, because at this point the dogfight was so close to start time that the neighborhood children have erected bleachers and are selling refreshments. And *somehow* through a combination of menacing faces and jerky movements you also inspire the strange dog to head off on his own down the street.

Okay, take a deep breath. Everything is fine. Harmony is once again restored. And now, it's finally time to "go for a walk" on this balmy summer day. Except this time a squirrel scampers by somewhere behind you, although you're not quite sure where. Both dogs pick a different angle of approach in their high-speed attempts to apprehend and kill him. Now suddenly you are wrapped in two leashes, each tightly wound around a different leg so that you look like some kind of overdressed, poorly planned bondage pictorial. And in the heat of the moment you are knocked to your knees and pulled forward toward a blind turn where none of the motorists speeding by will even be able to focus on you before they feel you beneath their tires. You know you have to get out of there fast, but you can't move either of your legs. And now your knees are scraped for the first time since you were seven.

"ASSHOLES! I SAID STAY!" you yell at your dogs, praying they accidentally decide to listen. It's happened before. If only it would happen again now. And magically, at the very last moment before you are meaninglessly mowed down by a well-meaning driver—a sacrifice at the shrine of dog recreation—*bingo*! They do! They actually STAY!!! Long enough for you to loosen the leather bindings from around your legs and get yourself back on your feet. And as you do, remind yourself of the incredible elegance of Newtonian physics. For every action there is an equal and opposite reaction. Yes! Everything synched up in a big cosmic tango.

But now your knees are bleeding and stinging so you gather the leashes tightly and march those two ungrateful animals back to the house, trying to remember to marvel at the uncomprehending, resilient expressions of joy they wear on their faces in spite of everything that has happened. You were almost killed. But as far as they are concerned, everything went very well.

Back in your home, you want to sit down in peace and quiet and bandage your knees—at least take a moment to recover from the trauma of a near-death experience. But of course the first thing you run into are the faces of the other two dogs who have done nothing since they saw you last but mourn your departure. Every molecule of their beings is alive with eager anticipation of the incredible good time they know you are going to show them. Oh well. Now you have no choice but to hook each of them up to a leash and repeat the entire process again with an all-new cast.

And this time, try to do it with more serenity, damn it.

12,000 Square Feet of Fun

I guess one of the really great things about living in Los Angeles is that you're only a three-hour drive from a whole other country. I say this kind of tentatively because I've lived here on and off for ten years and have never actually made the drive across the border. Plus, when I mentioned my intentions to do so to my so-called friends, they all came up with excuses as to why they couldn't join me. Everyone did warn me, however, of the reasons to buy Mexican auto insurance, which is why I left my car in a big parking lot north of the border and headed into Tijuana on foot.

After passing through a turnstile into a dank cement corridor, the observant pedestrian immediately notices that all the garbage cans are labeled PRODUTSA. Voilà! Just like magic! You're in a whole other country! (But I probably shouldn't overstate the "magic" part of the experience, because the most magical thing about the cement corridor down which you find yourself strolling is a little stand selling Fresh Baja Shrimp Cocktails—a proposition that seems less than completely appealing, for the same reason that fresh shrimp never look all that good on sale at the bus depot.)

At this point, the pedestrian may select from a bevy of variously priced cab rides. I pick a $3 ride with a white-haired man in a pin-striped suit who looks like Cesar Romero would look after recovering from a debilitating illness. He drops me off in lovely midtown Tijuana, in front of Woolworth de Mexico, where a big sign proclaims EVERYONE'S FAVORITE! PIE À LA MODE! Inside at the lunch counter are those four elderly white people Woolworth apparently keeps on retainer and sends from town to town, paying them handsomely to sit and drink coffee.

Ah, Tijuana, where on every corner you can be photographed with a burro that someone has painted to look like a zebra. Tijuana, with its multitude of stores and stalls and arcades where you can purchase inexpensive items of no particular value or use. Like those jumbo-size paintings on velvet of Eddie Murphy and Prince and Madonna. A guy tells me they cost "sixty-eight dollars with the frame, or . . . how much you feel you'd like to spend, lady?" thus opening up a philosophical mind-bender similar to the one about the tree that falls in the forest and may or may not make a sound. What *is* the proper price to pay for a painting on velvet of Eddie Murphy? Pondering this, I move on to a giant bin of brightly colored automatic switchblades, which appear to be a good buy at $2.99 apiece, although I can't be too sure because I've never priced automatic switchblades before. (But I do purchase a dozen because it occurs to me they'll make awfully good stocking stuffers. And by the way, Tijuana is definitely *the* place for all your hideous-marionette needs. At no more than $2.50 apiece, they're an excellent buy.)

I exit this store and enter another one, and then exit and enter a series of stores so identical that I suspect the Tijuana Chamber of Commerce is trying to make me feel as though I am going insane, much as the guy did to his wife in the movie *Gaslight.* And out in front of each store there appears to be the same guy calling out to me, "Lady! This is the place!"

I find myself following a blond kid of about seventeen dressed in tan shorts and flip-flops. "She said she'd do *anything,*" I hear him telling his demographically similar buddy. "*Really?* That's what she *said*?" the buddy replies as they both stop in front of a store window. "Those bongs are so rad. My parents got one just like that." We all walk in, past a large display of "pre-Columbian art" for $9.95. Inside the store I see two identically dressed identical twins (female) in their early sixties, each purchasing a bottle of Anaïs Anaïs. In the back of the store, just inches from the largest grouping of ceramic Little Bo Peeps I have ever seen, are clusters of pasty-faced Americans eating at dingy tables. And in the center of the store is a sign with an arrow indicating a descending flight of stairs and proclaiming 12,000 SQUARE FEET OF FUN! At the base of the stairs is a door, and from behind it comes the piercing shriek of gym whistles, my first acquaintance with "poppers"—a Tijuana custom wherein a restaurant patron has straight tequila poured into his or her mouth by a jovial waiter who is also blowing a whistle.

I am the sort of person who feels uncomfortable eating alone in a restaurant, and I've never been around more than 8,000 square feet of fun before, so as I begin my afternoon of solitary bar-hopping in Tijuana I realize I am taking some kind of significant developmental leap (although I've still not exactly determined in which direction). Many of the patio/

restaurant/bar hangouts I visit are on sunlit rooftops and seem to have their fair share of guys who look like Bruce Willis on a bender. Everywhere, Tiffany-style disco music blares and clusters of people lean toward one another and act stupid while someone else takes their picture. I sit down next to a table full of blond girls who could model for a painting that would be called *The Three Ages of Sharon Stone*. When the waiter comes over to inflict the dreaded poppers, one of them giggles too hard and gets her shot of tequila right in the eye.

Nearby, a Bruce Willis and his friend, a Bryant Gumbel, good-naturedly agree to dance with two notably older ladies who make me feel embarrassed for them by their very big, self-conscious I'm-sure-a-lively-older-gal-aren't-I? dance movements.

As far as I can tell, I am the only unaccompanied person of either sex in all of Tijuana's bars. At the Tequila Circus, however, some of the chairs are molded plastic clowns adorned with horrifically bright, smiling faces, so a single gal like me can appear to be enjoying a glass of beer on the lap of a psychotic circus performer. Across the street, People's: The Happiness and Joy Disco is done in a neo-Flintstonian motif. DANCE BACK ON TIME says the flashing sign as people I suspect might be shills try to encourage others to participate by boogying their brains out on the dance floor. This, by the way, is what happens when you accumulate some time in Tijuana— you begin to get a very definite sense that things are not at all what they seem.

Downstairs at the extremely crowded Tijuana Tilly's, I am reunited with my friends the multiple blond girls—each of whom is now dancing seductively with one of a matching set of suave black dudes. I've heard it said that you can tell if a person is good in bed by the way he or she behaves on the dance floor. Not being a dancer myself (and quite frankly, never having dated anyone who was), I cannot confirm or deny the validity of this theory, but if we presume it to be true, the three blond girls have met up with the only dancers in Tijuana who definitely do *not* have a sexual dysfunction.

By now the harsh light of the late Sunday afternoon sun has made these "fun" college kids sucking down their shots of tequila look like the tired middle-aged businessmen and women they are destined to become. So I head back to the street to catch a cab. On my way I pass a storefront that says MARRIAGES AND DIVORCES. "May I help you, lady?" asks a guy out front as I take a peek inside. "No, I'm just looking," I say. "Want to get married? Let's get married," he suggests, and as flattered as I am, I realize it's time to head home.

Taking one last pass through the stores, I notice with pleasure that whips are on sale for only $11.95, which I think is a darn good price, although I'm not sure because I've never priced any whips stateside (however, I do go ahead and purchase half a dozen since I *know* these will make good stocking stuffers).

Talk about inflation! My taxi driver tells me the ride back to the cement corridor will cost *five* dollars! Even though I'm not the sort of person who likes to barter for things, I do manage to get him down to three. But then when I get out of the car goofiness overtakes me and I decide to give him five anyway. Okay, I'm an idiot, but I figure he has to keep driving around Tijuana while I get to go home. Which is exactly what I did.

Greeting Disorder

One afternoon, having arrived home in a bad mood after a long series of thankless chores, it occurred to me that it was time to confront my dogs about an issue between us that was building to insurmountable proportions. I called for the two largest ones, Lewis and Tex, to join me in my office. Since they never come when I call, the two others arrived. I locked them in there and cornered Lewis and Tex in the front room, where we finally thrashed the whole thing out.

Me: Okay, you two, listen carefully. In the future it is
neither necessary nor desirable for you to greet me
every single time I walk in the door. Unless a minimum of two hours has passed, the previous greeting is
still in effect. In other words, if I come *in* the door,
and you greet me, and then several minutes later I go
out the door, only to return in a matter of seconds,
you do *not* have to greet me again.

Lewis: Ha-ha. Good one.

Me: I am serious. Maybe it would be best at this point to discuss the *purpose* of a greeting.

Tex: What is she talking about?

Lewis: Play along. We don't eat for about an hour.

Me: A *greeting* is what you give someone you have not seen *in a while*. A *while* is a period of time of more than two hours. Try another example. I come in the door after a day of work . . .

Tex: I would be so glad to see you that I would rush up and hurl myself at you. Then I would get up on my back legs, knocking you over, causing you to drop whatever you were carrying . . .

Lewis: Listen to what you're saying, bro. You know we're not supposed to get *up* on her.

Me: Very good, Lewis. Thank you.

Lewis: Which is why the approach *I* take is to circle closely, using body blocks. Throwing my whole weight against her legs so that she falls over and drops everything. Same exact result. I never have to get *up* on her at all.

Me: You're missing the point. All that is required from a greeting is a simple show of enthusiasm. Eyes filled with a certain amount of joy, a bit of tail-wagging. *That's it.*

Tex: What did she say?

Lewis: Just go with it. She likes to hear herself talk.

Me: Now that we've defined a greeting . . .

Lewis: And by the way, I like to make mine last until she's down on her knees, if not flat on her back . . .

Tex: I've seen your work, buddy. You're an artist.

Me: . . . Let's try one more exercise to see if you are getting the point. Okay. Imagine this. I decide to take out the garbage. I walk to the door . . .

Lewis: I'm right there with you.

Tex: I beat you there.

Lewis: The hell you do.

Me: I exit. About eight seconds later I come back *in* the door. What would be your response?

Tex: I'd be so thrilled to see you that I'd run up to you, hurl myself at you, then I'd get up on my back legs and . . .

Lewis: Dolt. You don't listen. We just went through this a second ago. It's circle and hurl, circle and lean . . . and hurl. Circle and hurl.

Me: *Stop!* Listen to me! The point was that you do not have to greet me again. You just greeted me seconds before. I'm sorry if this seems confusing but I'd like you just to blindly accept this rule and obey it. *Do not greet me every time I come in the door.*

Lewis: So you're asking us to be rude.

Tex: No, no, I hear you. Tell me if I've got it straight. You go *out* the door, and then you come *right back in*. We do *not* get up on you. No. We circle and hurl, circle and lean and hurl . . .

Lewis: There you go. Step on her feet and trip her. Tangle her up, and lean on her and at the same time circle . . .

Tex: I can definitely do that.

Lewis: Where is she going?

Tex: Looks like the bedroom. Whoa. She closed the door. How long is she going to be gone?

Lewis: I don't know. All I know is suddenly we're very alone.

Tex: How long has it been since we saw her?

Lewis: I don't know. A month? A year?

Tex: Wait! The door is opening. Oh my God! She's back!

Lewis: Dear God, thank you! She's back! Welcome back!

Tex: Come let me get up on you and give you a nice big kiss.

Deranged Love Mutants: The Story of Romeo and Juliet

Every year when Valentine's Day rolls around, I make a special point of trying to scan the horizon for a reasonable example of romantic love, just so I know what we're all supposed to be celebrating.

Of course, the preceding 364 days I am adrift in a sea of stories about love gone dopey. I refer here to both the whining weepy anecdotes of my various friends as well as those of the never-ending parade of deranged love mutants booked in triplicate on the afternoon talk shows. To say nothing of the stream of stunning examples reported daily.

My favorite:

A 71-year-old woman was arrested Friday after she allegedly doused her husband of more than 30 years with rubbing alcohol and set him on fire for eating a chocolate Easter bunny she had saved for herself, police said.

Proving once and for all that when evaluating the success of a love relationship, the element of longevity should not necessarily be the key.

But if *that* isn't, what is? It has become increasingly disturbing how few good models of love there are.

This year, we can't look to the First Couple for any hints. It's pretty apparent that Hillary is just putting the best face on some kind of marital sciatica. In fact, these past few years every single public couple who ever looked the least bit intriguing bought a ticket for the long slow ride to hell.

I still remember with a shudder when I thought Woody Allen and Mia Farrow looked like they had worked out something impressive. Eccentric, yes, but romantic and mature. That was way back in the late eighties—when we used to be able to count on England's royal couples to at least fake a show of romance.

This year, we can't even count on Tom and Roseanne. Yes, John Tesh and Connie Sellecca would *like* to step up to the plate as our new romantic ideal, but having survived the taping of an embarrassing infomercial is *not* qualification enough.

So this year, in honor of Valentine's Day, I decided to reread a true classic—*Romeo and Juliet.*

If you have not had the occasion to do so lately, please allow me to reacquaint you with the details of this timeless model of romantic love.

When we first meet the teenage Romeo, it is a Sunday night and he has decided to crash a ball just to catch a glimpse of Rosaline, a girl with whom he is desperately in love. Instead, he meets the thirteen-year-old Juliet. And even though only seconds before he was deeply in love with Rosaline, *now* he knows *instantly* that this thirteen-year-old girl is the greatest love of his life. Really. She is. He's not kidding this time.

Juliet has never been in love before. And yes, their two families hate each other. But so what? My parents never liked anyone I went out with either. The important thing is that by Monday afternoon, so beautiful is their love, they go ahead and get married.

Just one day later.

In lieu of a honeymoon, Romeo kills Juliet's cousin and Juliet goes back home to spend the night at her parents' house. Of course her parents do not know about the marriage yet, but they are so beside themselves with grief about the murdered cousin that Juliet's father decides there is no time like the present to arrange for Juliet to marry an older man.

Well, she *is* thirteen and not getting any younger. Soon, she'll be thirteen and a half. However, because he's an adult and not a hotheaded teenager, he really doesn't want to rush things. So he sets the wedding date for Thursday.

Naturally, the already-married Juliet realizes she must defy her father's wishes. She is no longer a codependent. She has boundaries and as a fully *individualized* adult, she must stand up to him and tell him her intentions. She takes the most sensible course of action under the circumstances. She pretends to be dead.

This also bodes very well for the future of her marriage to Romeo since we now know that the core of any "love at first sight" attraction is usually "repetition compulsion"—wherein a person reenacts the identical behavior and problems first seen in the parent-child relationship.

Thank God both Romeo and Juliet killed themselves before we were able to chart their marriage any further into the future, when it most certainly would have descended into scenarios like this:

(*Romeo enters parlor*)

"Juliet! Juliet! My light! I'm home! Juliet? Oh, I forgot to tell you that I ate that chocolate Easter bunny that you were . . . Juliet? Juliet? Oh no. Honey. Not dead again. Don't tell me you're dead again. Please don't be playing dead again. You were just dead on Monday. I can't call 911 twice in one week. It's too embarrassing. Juliet? Juliet?"

Well, there you have this year's Valentine's Day poster couple. A thirteen-year-old girl who likes to pretend to be dead married to a teenage murderer who has no trouble falling in love with two different girls on the same Sunday night.

Which leaves us with this slightly comforting fact:

There is no reason to lament today's lack of viable romantic models. Things are no worse now than they ever were. The only difference is that back then no one watched Oprah or read psychology books. So they didn't mind calling deranged neurotic behavior "the greatest love story ever told."

Happy Valentine's Day.

Viva Las Wine Goddesses!

So the other weekend I went to Las Vegas on a date. At first I had my doubts about our choice of venue, and consulted friends, who fell into two camps: those who found the excesses and depravities of the place to be the very definition of hilarity and those for whom the identical elements were at the heart of a searing existential depression, which, they felt, could only lead to a loss of the will to live.

I can confirm that there is real truth to both perceptions, and it seems to me that the best way to avoid passing from the first camp to the second is to be very careful about the length of your stay. *This must not,* for any sensitive and reasonably intelligent adult, *exceed thirty-six hours.* For those of us blessed (or cursed) with a hyperactive sense of the ironic, Las Vegas, taken in small doses, is a specialty act without peer. And so I present you now with a kind of handy guidebook for your own short visit. Think of it as something you might get from that *big* travel writer—I forget his name—the one who writes all the "Rome on five dollars a day" things, if he weren't too big a weenie to write it.

Merrill's Guide to Thirty-six Hours of Vegas Fun

Las Vegas is but a hop, a skip, and a jump from Los Angeles. But since fewer and fewer people rely on any of the above for their transportational needs, you have your choice of flying or driving. We drove—through mile after mile of pale orange landscape, dotted with tiny specks of black and pale green that are either sagebrush or tumbleweed or rock—until we reached Las Vegas.

Of course everyone knows what the Las Vegas strip looks like from a million movies and videotape montages. But they ill prepare you for how really, really bizarre it is in three dimensions. Almost everywhere you look, a building is screaming a visual or verbal insanity at you. The overall effect is of something you made up in a feverish dream one night when you drank too much tequila and ate too many pepperoncini.

Tip Number 1: Stay at the Gaudiest Hotel You Can Afford. Why? Because the whole point of going to Las Vegas is to have the Las Vegasiest time you can have. I heartily recommend Caesars Palace, which I found to be the wackiest luxury hotel that I have ever been in, around, or near. It's not just because the employees wear costumes or because of all the oversize antiquities, friezes, and historical references. How about those moving sidewalks that carry you into the complex—passing through a miniature temple type of structure, with gold columns and horns to announce your arrival—and then abandon you to the regular old stationary sidewalks for your exit?

Many movies, such as *Rain Man,* have shown us in loving detail the lavish suites full of grand pianos and chandeliers that are provided for the high rollers. We, however, had an economy-priced room right next to food services, just a short distance down the hall from accounting. This simple room did not have even a regular-size piano, but it did feature a giant raised marble bathtub. Okay, fine, I can definitely follow the concept of a giant raised marble bathtub/shower combo, but the concept kind of goes south in the small economy rooms where the tub has to serve instead of a stall shower. And since these tubs are located nearly in the center of the floor—only feet from the bed and the TV and the window—suddenly you are faced with a far-from-glamorous situation, namely, one where bathing must be done in the presence of all people in the room. This is less than ideal, *especially* if you happen to be sharing a hotel room with someone you barely know.

Now you might be muttering to yourself, "What kind of moron would share a hotel room with someone she barely knows?" but that is not something I want to discuss. This is, after all, my essay. The point I am making here is that maybe you never need to know someone so well that you lose altogether the option of showering privately. And in this particular room, your roommate, who may be pretending to sleep or watch TV, is, unquestionably, just watching you shower.

Which brings us to the in-house viewing selections. There was a tape showcasing the various wining and dining opportunities in our very own hotel complex, such as "Cleopatra's Barge" for dancing and "The Bacchanal Room," where you dine in splendor, served by the lovely "wine goddesses." There was also a learn-to-gamble-with-Larry-Manetti tape that my date must have watched about 300 times. In this, a blond woman in a fur and the older guy from *Magnum P.I.* who is not Tom Selleck take some pointers from Larry Manetti (I forget just who he is). But in a hilarious twist of fate they end up beating him at his own game . . . and then the fun begins!!!! Once your sides have stopped aching from laughter (and once you have gotten over the shock of showering in front of someone who doesn't mind watching Larry Manetti for hours on end), it's high time to get the hell out of the room and experience some of that world-famous Las Vegas nightlife!

Tip Number 2: Go to a Show. Somewhere in your room is a book that lists every show in town. I selected *Nudes on Ice* for our viewing enjoyment because . . . well, it was the stupidest-sounding show available. Now, I realize that not everyone selects their entertainment according to this criterion (and, by the way, aren't you glad you don't have to travel with me?), but everything on the list sounded pretty stupid to me, so I felt that attending the stupidest one of them all would be the most Las Vegasy thing to do. (I actually came very close to selecting *Boylesque,* but in the end I felt that Las Vegas men pretending to be women would be less interesting than the men pretending to be men and the women pretending to be women.) And I was not disappointed. I don't know whether or not partially nude women so bored with their jobs that they could barely keep their cigarette butts lit constitutes a "sexsational revue" (as the program advertised), but it was interesting to note that the more breast was exposed, the less skating was required. I guess this equation is relevant in every walk of life.

Especially memorable for me was Act 5, which was called

"A Russian Fantasy" and which seemed to my nonexpert eyes to be a re-creation of that period of Russian history when, because of a crop shortage or something, the czar apparently decreed that only a percentage of women in the royal court could be fully dressed.

Honorable mention goes to the comedian who came out and devoted a third of his act to dirty balloon animals (always a rollicking good time). This is entertainment that you cannot see anywhere else in the world, and for a very good reason. Why in the world would you want to?

Tip Number 3: Win a Bunch of Money. Let me begin this section by saying that I have never been remotely interested in gambling. I have always felt that nothing ventured is nothing lost. I have never been able to see the fun in losing $5 and then winning back $3.50. Which gives you an idea of the kind of stakes I usually play. But, influenced by my date, I picked the right number at roulette and immediately won $400. And before the evening was over, we had won $1,200. I cannot recommend this too highly. If it hasn't occurred to you, win $1,200 and see for yourself. It's very energizing and really adds to your Vegas fun.

Tip Number 4: Dine Among the Wine Goddesses. By now you will have seen the ad on your color TV (while you were trying not to watch someone else shower). What sort of Las Vegas visitor would you be if you didn't give the wine goddesses their due? At least, this was my rap right up until we were seated at our table and I saw the wine goddesses in diaphanous harem outfits circling my date, offering to give him some kind of theoretical eye massage. Maybe I wouldn't have gotten quite so ticked off if there had been wine gods available for the gals. Maybe then we all could have had a great big laugh about it. Ha, ha, ha. As it was, I, for the first time in my life, felt it necessary to threaten restaurant help with my Swiss Army knife.

There were other highlights to the meal besides the much-loathed wine goddesses. For instance, it's not every restaurant that offers you what look like 3-D fiberglass replicas of the available entrées to examine before you order. For those of us who have never actually seen what a real veal chop looks like, this is extraordinarily helpful. But the biggest dinner highlight was definitely the arrival of Julius Caesar and Cleopatra, heralded by the crash of a giant gong. Dressed in full historical regalia, this important couple had come all the way through time with nothing more on their minds than to find out how we were enjoying our meal. And I confess I tried to use what little clout I had with the great Roman emperor to see about getting the wine goddesses pulled off the face of the earth.

Tip Number 5: On Your Way Out of Town, Be Sure to Visit the Liberace Museum. Now, I don't want to say too much here. I know the man came to a tragic end. But let me just suggest that you slow down while passing through the portion of the museum devoted to Lee's brother George, and observe that in a glass case both his driver's license and his frequent flier card have been mounted and preserved. On sale in the gift shop are a variety of swell items. Because I was ahead my half of the $1,200, I was able to purchase the Liberace paper clips, the coffee mug, the photo-embossed Christmas ornament, the key chain, the extra-large postcard of Liberace posing by his closet, and the box of scented soaps, each shaped like a grand piano and emblazoned with his name.

Tip Number 6: Now Get Out of There and Don't Look Back. And so we say good-bye to the city of Las Vegas, remembering that we'd better not overstay our thirty-six hours. Taking with us a whole lot of free money and a bunch of silly stuff . . . and leaving behind the goddamn wine goddesses. And they'd better stay the hell out of Los Angeles if they know what's good for them.

Pets and
the Single Girl

Being a single woman and living by yourself in the United States of America can be a very rough life. Okay . . . it's a pretty loose definition of the word "rough." It's not "rough" like living in Bosnia and dodging mortar fire. Or Russia in the midst of economic and cultural collapse. Or doing anything at all in Somalia or the Sudan. Come to think of it, it's not even "rough" like trying to be a single mother in *this* country. Or being half of one of those ghastly couples who are making a public descent into hell, like Ben and Jen or Britney and her latest husband. Or even part of any less publicized troubled couple, like the ones who call day and night on those radio psychology shows or turn up on *Jerry Springer.* I guess what I'm actually saying here is that being a single woman and living by yourself in the United States of America is a pretty easy hand to play.

After all, you don't have to debate your every decision with a critical detractor; there's no one around to constantly remind you which of your habits make others insane. You don't have to cook if you don't want to. And then on the other hand, if you want to eat shamelessly and endlessly, there is no one to comment, "Geez, you sure pack it away." You can decorate eccentrically. You can hang around with worthless weasels and ne'er-do-wells. Overall, it's a relatively painless way of life. Sure, you have to attend to every exasperating detail of your day all by yourself. But come on—that's a small price to pay. In fact, maybe it's *too* small. Maybe things are just a little bit too easy.

When my dog Stan died, there were a couple of weeks when I lived pet-free. I fantasized that finally not being tied down to a dependent would give my spontaneous nature a chance to grow and flower. Then I realized that not only didn't I have much of a spontaneous nature but that the reason I wasn't partaking of the constant barrage of interesting activities and social events all around me was because I was a lazy ne'er-do-well. Eventually this caused me to see myself in such an unflattering light that I had no choice but to go straight to the pound and come home with a puppy. And since that time, I have never had to look my own inadequacies squarely in the eye again because I have been blessed by the constant inconveniences of pet ownership. Which brings me to our topic here today:

The Importance of Pets for Single Women

I. A Bottomless Source of Guilt

A good, loving pet can provide his or her owner with reasons to feel guilty pretty much twenty-four hours a day—something that might be in short supply for the happy-go-lucky single woman. I have four dogs and every time I shift in my chair one of them gets up and runs to the door, wearing an expression on his face that reminds me of a small child on Christmas morning. If he could talk (and thank *God* he can't; I'm really not up to hearing him go on about butt itch) he would be saying: "Are you ready to go? You need a few seconds? Fine. I'll wait right here. Lalala two three four. How about *now*? No? Take your time. No problem. What about NOW? Okay. Fine. How about *NOW*?" And there I sit, knowing that while at no point did I have any intention of going anywhere, my cavalier lack of specific recreational intentions seems to have caused several creatures, whose only purpose in life is to show me constant love, intense disappointment if not searing depression.

And then, to make matters even worse, how about those occasions when I *do* have intentions to go somewhere but for wacky, selfish reasons of my own am planning to make the excursion unaccompanied by dogs? Now suddenly I am confronted with a sea of demoralized faces, silently blocking my path to the door, mouths agape as they beg me to reconsider the consequences of my actions. "You wouldn't enjoy yourself at my dentist," I explain to them. "The magazines are old. *No* dogs go to the dentist. Don't feel hurt. *No one wants* to get fitted for crowns," I say as I squeeze through the door with a heavy heart, wondering what kind of callow, unfeeling slob I am after all . . . only to return several hours later—tired and grumpy and sore—to be greeted by dogs who are *really* ready to go somewhere *now. Anywhere.* And this time they are *really not kidding.*

II. Dietary Benefits

When you are single you tend to lapse into eating patterns that can be self-indulgent. But when you are a pet owner you never again have to worry about consuming a lot of empty calories because the motto of any self-respecting pet of any sort (in fact, a lot of them have it embroidered on pillows) is "Please. I'm starving. Let me have *all* of what you are eating right *now*." To eat in the presence of most dogs is an experience not unlike sitting down to a picnic lunch in Bangladesh. And quite frankly, nothing puts a damper on the old appetite like many pairs of pleading, desperate eyes riveted to your every fork and mouth movement. This is something most pets are willing to do for you at all times, *regardless* of how recently they have been fed, thus enabling any reasonably sensitive person to lose three to five pounds a week with ease.

III. Practice for Living with a Significant Other

Living with an actual man can have a variety of dangerous side effects. He can break your heart, threaten your sanity and your physical well-being, and cause you numerous personal and professional dysfunctions that can take years of costly and time-consuming therapy to unravel. So you don't want to mess with the wrong man: You have to choose your shots very carefully. On the other hand, you don't want to get so enamored of your own company that you get out of practice entirely and possibly lose the desire to cohabit. (Or do you? For the sake of argument, let's *say* you don't.) Pets can help to provide you with many of the same irritants that living with the man of your dreams will entail.

For instance, one of the hallmarks of every serious relationship I have had with a man has been uncomfortable sleeping circumstances. By this I refer to the cramped positions and rasping mouth noises that sleeping with a large unwieldy human male can often involve. And these inconveniences are cheerfully duplicated by any pet that you allow to share your bed (which in my case is every pet I have ever had). At first it is cozy and cuddly and cute—just like with a guy. And then, like with a guy, they fall asleep in some unlikely-looking position—adorable, trusting, and peaceful. And even as all the feeling in your legs begins to vanish, you are reluctant to wake them. When at last you do try to shift because you feel as though you may have severed your spinal cord, you realize that it is now impossible because they are dead weight—no easier to budge than a giant sack of lawn clippings. And so you wake the next morning, feeling as though you have been through hip replacement surgery, happy in the knowledge that your furry little pal hasn't missed any of his or her mandatory twenty-two-hours-a-day sleep.

IV. Practice for Being a Parent

Before a woman takes on the enormous responsibility of parenting, is it not a good idea to do a test run? This is where raising a pet can provide some interesting data. For instance, my dog Lewis, who is the only creature on the planet who truly reflects my influence (because he has lived with me since he was only six weeks old), is an overweight, whiny, badly groomed, poorly behaved, inconsiderate, and pointlessly defiant giant boy who drools constantly and has incredibly high self-esteem. And so I have learned that any child of mine may well turn out to be an annoying big fat dumb guy who has no respect for the rights of others.

Lewis is currently dating one of my couches and seems to care nothing at all about the fact that he is also destroying the object of his affection in the process. This teaches me that I have also managed to duplicate in my dog the kind of behavior I have come to expect from the men I date. I don't know what the horrifying Freudian truth behind this fact might be, but I do know this: It would be in the best interests of everyone concerned for the government to pay me a monthly subsidy *not* to ever have children (much as they pay certain farmers not to grow crops). I think we all have quite enough to worry about as it is.

V. A Flawless All-purpose Excuse

When you are single you find yourself getting talked into attending a lot of functions you would avoid if you had any kind of *real* life. To say nothing of the potentially nightmarish circumstances provided by dating. In which case "I have to get home and let out my dog" will serve you much better and be kinder to say than "If I have to sit here and listen to one more tedious phrase tumble out of your big rubbery head I think I'm going to have to start taking hostages."

So—summing up—pet ownership offers the willing single woman a wonderful world of experiences and opportunities. At least that's what I keep telling myself when I wonder what in the world I've gotten myself into.

A Little Intimate Exploration

Last week I had to go to Boston on a business trip.

I stayed in Cambridge, in a pretty hotel right on Harvard Square. Never having been to the area before, I had certain preconceived notions about New England being a more conservative, more tradition-oriented-type of place than my constantly ridiculed homeland of Los Angeles.

However, I had an experience on my second night that turned my notion of New England on its ear. It also made me think I understand men even *less* than I had previously not understood them.

First, I should say that I hate staying in hotels alone. I wake up all night long, *starving* as though I haven't eaten for weeks. The selection of foods for sale in what they laughingly refer to as the Refreshment Center is a diet-conscious person's nightmare: Snickers, Pringles, honey-glazed peanuts, a small vacuum-sealed can of macadamia nuts (43 million calories, economically priced at $19.95).

Yes, yes, I know, I could call room service, but that means a twenty-five-minute wait and guarantees finally falling back to sleep twenty seconds before that frightening wake-up call rings through.

So, with these concerns in mind, I made a special note to myself during check-in when I saw the giant bowl of apples in the lobby. *Hmm,* I thought, *I could stash a couple on the nightstand and then have something sensible to snack on when I wake up.*

Which is why, on evening two, I was headed down to the lobby at eleven at night wearing blue sweatpants and a pink sweater, my hair pinned on top of my head in a barrette. I had a brief discussion with myself re: "Am I too slobby for the lobby?" But then I answered, "No, I'm fine. I will dash in and out of the elevator, fleet as the wind. I will be but a fruit-bearing apparition."

So down the elevator I rode. But when I returned, wielding apples, I noticed there was a casually dressed middle-aged white man already on board. Average-looking. No apparent disfiguring scars or frightening facial deformities.

Like most women, I have a moment's hesitation when I get into an elevator with a man I don't know. But this being a fairly expensive hotel, I wasn't too concerned, even though, as we began ascending, I had the feeling he was looking at me too intently. However, I have been reluctant to make any assumptions since the time at the bookstore when I sensed that a man was staring at me. I was assembling my face into a frosty expression to indicate that I was far too busy for the likes of him when he leaned over and whispered in my ear, "Your dress is on inside out." Looking down, I noticed that the interior seams of my stretchy black dress were in fact exposed. "I *know*," I said with a world-weary haughtiness meant to imply that I sometimes *preferred* to wear my dress inside out.

Then, once he left, I made a beeline for the ladies' room.

So I wasn't going to draw any overly quick conclusions about Elevator Guy until he started talking to me.

"Are you interested in a little intimate exploration?" he said offhandedly.

"Excuse me?" I answered.

For a minute I thought "intimate exploration" might be code for some quasi-religious cult that would teach me to chant "Nam myoho renge kyo" and the next thing I knew, I would owe $30,000 and have to hire a deprogrammer.

"What does that mean?" I asked him.

"Sex," he said.

Now my jaw hit my knees. My internal alarm systems all started blaring to me. *Get off the elevator. Get away from this guy.*

"No!" I said to him. "No. No. No!"

The elevator doors opened. I exited. So did he.

The doors shut behind us. There we were, together, both of us on *his* floor.

"I find you very attractive," he continued.

"Thank you," I said reflexively, heading down a hallway to no place in particular, "that's very kind of you. Thanks a lot."

("Was I really just thanking a man who I was scared was a psycho rapist?" I asked myself as I looked for some other way to get back to my room.)

Once I was in my room a few minutes later, alone and eating an apple, the questions started flooding my brain.

Why did this happen? Was this guy riding the elevator at

eleven at night waiting for *any* living breathing single female to get on board so he could ask this question? Or was there something about *me* and *my demeanor* that made this guy think I'd be interested? Did my sweatpants and sweater say something slutty? Is this how the prostitutes operated in Harvard Square? Did they work the hotel elevators dressed in sweatpants?

"No," said my friend Andy, "if he thought you were a prostitute he would have asked, 'How much?' In which case you could have answered, 'Two apples.'"

Ultimately, it was the abrupt nature of the request that was so shocking. Had he said to me, "The bars are still open. Can I buy you a drink?" I *still* would have said no, but I would have thought of his behavior as making sense in the American culture as I have come to know it.

Once when I was in college, at UC Berkeley, a similar thing happened. A preppy-looking white guy in his twenties followed me to my car. "I'd really like to f— you," he said to me. No offer of a drink or a movie and dinner here either. "Oh, uh, okay. Thanks a lot," I replied, getting into my car so quickly my land speed record for door locking has never been meaningfully challenged. (Perhaps this was where my tradition of thanking a would-be rapist started.)

But that was, after all, the early seventies, on a college campus. My "gentleman caller" looked like the kind of delusional accounting student who had taken some advice from a *Penthouse* letter that said, "Yeah, the college coeds *want* it, pal. Just go up to them and tell them and they'll go home with you."

The puzzling part about the other night was that this is *so* not the seventies, which raises the question "What was this guy *thinking*?" Had this *ever* worked for him? Are there women willing to go from zero to one hundred without even a warm-up hello? Was there ever a woman who said, "Hmm, intimate exploration! Sounds good! Your room or mine?"

And then I started to wonder, *Well, what if he'd been incredibly attractive? What if he'd been, say, Brad Pitt—well, what then?*

Of course, I still would have said no. But I bet I would have offered him one of my apples.

How to Please a Man Every Time and Have Him Okay Maybe Not Beg for More but at Least Not Demand a Whole Lot Less

Through my very special home-brewed blend of insecurity, moon blindness, and some sort of nonspecific mineral deficiency, I have spent much of my life totally unable to accurately read the sexual signals sent me by the opposite sex. So truly terrible am I at this, I have actually had men I invited into my home (after a pleasant evening out together) hanging around until three or four in the morning and still not been able to tell if it was safe to interpret their behavior as evidence of sexual interest. Perhaps, I would reason to myself, they are grateful to have found shelter and are harboring the delusion that if they hang in a while longer they might eventually receive some hot soup.

It always seemed to me that to presume anything more was to open myself up to the risk of a painful rejection. And thus, the only clue that such a date was actually interested in a physical encounter of any kind came after the man in question had passed out cold, having endured all he could stand of hours on end of my fascinating childhood reminiscences. Any subsequent attempts I might make to try to revive him would amount to the only contact that would ever take place.

Of course, that was the *old* me. Now I know better. Not because I have become more astute but because over the years I have had it repeatedly explained to me by numerous men of reasonable intelligence that the adult human male does *not* hang around endlessly in a place he does not want to be unless he has a sexual motive. I have been bluntly advised that it would be safe for me to go ahead and presume that any man exhibiting a willingness to listen to even *one* consecutive hour of my fascinating childhood stories is interested in more than just another hour of my fascinating childhood stories.

Okay. That understood, I have moved forward and developed a slick method of seductive maneuvering that can carry a person forward from that point.

Merrill's Five Steps to a Sexual Seduction

1. Offer him something to drink. It is, of course, incredibly important to remember to *have something drinkable somewhere on the premises.* How many were the times when I have made this offer only to discover, to my embarrassment, that the only remotely drinkable liquid in my refrigerator was a small amount of either canola oil or no-fat ranch-style dressing. And the truth is, even when served on the rocks in a lovely cut-glass crystal

goblet, neither one seems to get a very favorable
response.

2. This accomplished, next comes the old "Let me slip into
something more comfortable." This step, too, is fraught
with pitfalls if you, like me in most instances, make the
mistake of wearing something quite comfortable in the
first place. Now you are faced with the seemingly unsolv-
able dilemma of trying to find something *more* comfortable than the jeans and sweater you already have on.
Forget about anything you may have purchased from the
Victoria's Secret catalog. That stuff is all much less comfortable. Which is why you must commit to memory this
critical dating rule: Always wear something *uncomfortable*
out on a date. Only then can you really provide yourself
with the fullest range of eventual changing options.

3. Now sit down with your potential beloved on a piece of
furniture large enough for two and attempt to initiate a
seductive vibe through eye contact. The best way to kick
this off is to encourage him to talk about something *he*
finds fascinating—like why Ferraris are cooler than
Porsches. In many cases this will amount to something
you can barely pay attention to, but do not worry about
that because this type of man tends to feel that the act of
hearing himself talk about something of interest only to
him in fact constitutes having a conversation. The rest of
the good news is that later, when he thinks back on how
the evening went, he will recall that *you* were a really good
conversationalist!

4. Meanwhile, use this important downtime to begin recit-
ing silently that most powerful mantra of seduction—the

one that is virtually guaranteed to draw the attractive man of your dreams to you like malaria to a mosquito. Say it with me now: *Come here. Go away. Come here. Go away. I love you. I really don't want you. Come here. Go away. Come here. Go away.* For maximum effectiveness we must now borrow a page from that most successful group of seducers—the serial killers. Deranged? Nuts? Yes, absolutely, but never without willing sexual partners or a date on a Saturday night. Why? Well, perhaps it is that magnetic facial expression which seems to combine a radiant vulnerable loving smile with the detached gaze of a slaughterhouse foreman or a movie star on his way into a drug rehab program. *Why* this works is not important. It works, that's all we know. (In fact, we're all better off not knowing why it works, aren't we?)

5. How long should you keep this up? Well, if after a good hour nothing much seems to be happening, consult your watch and move on to the final powerful step. Wait for the first conversational lull and then jump in with both feet and begin to dominate with stories from your childhood. If, after twenty-five minutes, you find your date is still both present *and* feigning interest, assume he has the hots for you. Go ahead and make your move.

Postscript

Because not every completed seduction attempt leads to anything particularly pleasing I feel compelled to answer the following common question before it has even been asked:

Question: How many times should you allow a guy to slam your head into the wall behind your bed before you officially declare it "bad sex" and attempt to abort the proceedings?

Answer: Two. The first time, it is still possible that it was only an accident.

Hip, Pretentious L.A.

No one would argue that L.A. leads the country in opportunities for being hip and pretentious. But what is often overlooked is how many distinctly *different* ways to be pretentiously hip L.A. has to offer. Yes, yes, other cities all have an "in" spot or two. But within the borders of the greater Los Angeles area, there are multitudes of dissimilar kinds of pretentious "in" spots available to ensure that visitor and resident alike can experience the widest possible variety of ways to feel inadequate, inferior, irrelevant, and out of it.

Let's Start with Beverly Hills, of Course

There is no place like the streets of Beverly Hills to make people of every race, creed, religion, and nationality feel too large, too clunky, too poorly groomed. This section of the city offers such a well-worn path to self-loathing that even guests from faraway countries know to begin preparing themselves for that ugly, fat, and ill-at-ease feeling as soon as they get off the plane.

From the moment you join the matched set of impeccably detailed nouveau blondes nuzzling the maître d' at the Grill, you will find yourself surrounded by some of the most superficial and pointlessly judgmental humans in all the world. You are now in the midst of our nation's largest indigenous population of nature's most innately repellent creature: the professionally manicured male. The upside of this for you, the incipient diner, is that it works as a form of weight control since there is nothing like the sight of a little clear nail polish on the hands of a tanned, overgroomed, overperfumed, middle-aged heterosexual man to make a normal person lose their desire to eat.

Once you have settled at your table by the kitchen door, observe how many of the patrons here move in clusters from one table to the next, cooing as they extend suspiciously oversize greetings to people they may have seen earlier that very day. They are lawyers, agents, heads of production companies, assorted executives, producers, managers, and the new second or third wives or girlfriends of all of the above, and they are awash in very specific kinds of watches, purses, shoes, haircuts, jewelry, accessories, and brands of clothing the likes of which a status-symbol-impaired person such as myself could not identify if Jeffrey Katzenberg, Mike Ovitz, and Michael Eisner and all of their wives, past and present and future, threw fistfuls of them at me from now until Christmas.

The Sunset Strip: Another Place to Feel Like a Dork

A more complex but only slightly more original way to feel out of it is available at the hip and pretentious nightclubs and bars along the Sunset Strip. Welcome to the part of town where the idea of printing the name of the establishment somewhere visible is thought to be a laughable overstatement. If you are so out of it that you need to *see* the name of the place to which you are going, you do not deserve the privilege of feeling inadequate there.

Let's begin at the Bar Marmont, where the glittering transsexual maître d's set such an immediate standard of full-court hipness that you know immediately you will never be able to measure up, no matter how many times you think about going home to change outfits. The good news is that inside the bar the lighting is so low you will soon become the invisible person you desperately want to be.

Just a few doors down is the Standard, a big concrete structure that has had a real identity crisis since it was a retirement home in the eighties. The Standard *does* have its name printed on its marquee, only it's upside down! This pointless affectation will give you some idea of the rollicking good time that awaits you inside. Out in the driveway, you are greeted by a valet parking team all dressed in extremely puzzling, possibly demoralizing jockey outfits. Walk through the large glass doors, and notice that right behind the concierge desk is the Standard's signature piece of room décor: a large human-size aquarium in which a swimsuit-attired human reclines on a clear vinyl air mattress atop a layer of Astroturf. The other night it was a twentysomething spiky-haired male in boxer shorts and sunglasses, boogying visibly to a continuous loop of "Love to Love You Baby." He was also wearing inflatable dinosaur hands and feet to show he had personality plus, lest we get the impression that he was just some unemployed recent high school grad who probably hadn't even tried yet to explain his new part-time job to his parents.

Now it is your option to sit in one of the moderno furniture groupings and observe dinosaur boy's shiftings and repositionings as you wait a good half an hour for someone to take your drink order. Perhaps you will find it amusing to watch as the young, trendily dressed clientele try not to bump their heads on the low-hanging goosenecked lamps or trip on the retro shag carpeting. You will never have a better opportunity to observe clusters of moody young men slouching on fuzzy couches, preparing for the lifetime of watching television they know lies ahead! For a challenge, see if you can spot two females in a row on the line for the restroom who do *not* yet have breast implants. Or work on cultivating your patience as you realize you cannot leave because, even though you ordered your drink forty-five minutes ago, you gave the waitress your credit card. Now there is no sign of her anywhere. Does she even still work here?

Perhaps you'd like to go out to the patio, stare at the large inflatable starfish floating in the lighted pool, and contemplate whether the other people here are really having a fabulous time or are all just faking it.

Which brings us to the Sky Bar, a couple of doors down at the Mondrian Hotel, a place that will be forever distinct for me as the Sunset Strip location where I suffered the maximum amount of punishment for not being hip enough. I speak of the day I went there for an early dinner with a colleague from work. We were seated in a tiki-hut area, just off the pool, where we could watch as hotel staffers who looked like Milli Vanilli carrying spray bottles full of distilled water circulated amongst the swimsuited hotel guests to offer them a complimentary moistening in the name of better tanning.

Once my salad was delivered by a Pamela Anderson clone, I noticed that on the table in front of me were two condiment dishes: a container of salt and a small galvanized tureen of granules. As a longtime L.A. resident, I am only too well acquainted with our city's fixation on condiment reconfigurations: the fresh-ground-pepper mill versus the stale old pepper shaker; the grind-your-own-salt mill; the gigantic crystals of rock sugar; the small dishes of unidentified oils and sauces. So I said to myself, "Salt and a container of granules. Must be a hip new way to serve pepper." And I took a pinch between my thumb and forefinger and sprinkled it on my salad.

That is when I noticed that my colleague was *looking* at me funny. As I began eating, I realized I had a lot of sand on my salad. And so it came to pass that I learned that the small tureen of granules was not a hip new pepper-distributing system but a tureen of sand, intended for cigar night. I was so humiliated that I ate the salad anyway, pretending it had hardly any sand. Which of course was a lie. My tongue thought we were at the beach.

The other night, when I revisited the scene of my humiliation, it seemed to have gotten even more pretentious. I was prohibited from stepping into the tureen-of-sand area for lack of proper hotel ID by a haughty young male model wannabe stationed at a *troughlike BARRICADE OF WHEATGRASS*!!

Most Original Way to Feel
Out of It: Silverlake

Even though you may have felt too hip, too artsy, too alienated for the bars of the Sunset Strip, from the minute you enter one of the small—I am tempted to call them Mom-and-Pop establishments, but they are really more Mom and her weird third husband who fixes motorcycles—anyway, one of the small establishments in the heart of Silverlake, you will realize that you are not underground enough, not up to speed enough on alternative bands, not pierced or tattooed enough, not original enough in your choice of clothing. Now you are too mainstream.

Before social discomfort causes you to flee, Silverlake offers opportunities to feel ill at ease in some of Los Angeles's most artistic-looking rooms. Akbar, on Sunset, leads you from a very nondescript exterior to a very lush Middle Eastern–themed interior full of fezzes, hanging paper lights, and mosquelike architectural details, columns, arches. And men, men, men!

A few blocks away, the totally unlabeled Good Luck Bar, so named because that is what you need to find it, has a beautiful red interior, full of little lights, paper lanterns, and dark rooms with sofas better suited for making out than talking. It's so loud in there I suggest you bring a megaphone. There are, however, some very hip drinks, such as Ng Ka Py, a Chinese herb whiskey that tastes a little like licorice. But inebriation alone will not provide a sense of belonging.

Around the corner, the barely labeled Vida restaurant offers a unique chance to sit at a subterranean table and eat at the always desirable eye level with the floor. I think that one of the best indicators of a hip, pretentious place is menu language that is too embarrassing to say out loud when you order. The menu here is corny enough to convince you that you are at a bohemian-themed restaurant in Anaheim, next door to Medieval Times. There is a salad called Lettuce Entertain You and a soup called Flavor Flave, phrases a sensible person would never speak aloud.

From "too geeky for Beverly Hills" to "too alienated for the Sunset Strip" to "too mainstream for Silverlake," L.A. offers more reasons to just not bother going anywhere than *any city in the world*!! Those of us who are too lazy to go out anyway must bow our heads in a humble gesture of thanks.

One of the
Most Thrilling
Days of My Life

"People never say what they mean," the speaker tells us for the third time. He is a bug-eyed redhead in his early thirties named Peter Lowe and he is addressing what looks like a sellout crowd of several thousand people who have come to the L.A. Convention Center to attend "SUCCESS 2000. SEE YOU AT THE TOP!" We are here to learn "How to gain rapport with anyone . . . instantly!" and "How to turn dreams into reality." And we are as widely varied a group of humans as I have seen congregated in one place at one time since high school assembly. The black guy with the gold earring in the gray sweatshirt looks like a rapper. The woman in front of me in the dark green sport coat and scruffy half boots looks like a riding instructor. The blond woman across the aisle in the brown turtleneck knit dress and patterned nylons looks like a kindergarten teacher. The bulldog-faced guy in the tight sport coat seated behind her looks like . . . okay *he* looks like a salesman.

"It was one of the most thrilling days of my life," says Shirley Hartford of Century 21 right at the top of the advertisement that caught my attention in the *L.A. Times.* "What will *you* be saying after attending this dynamic event?" I can't wait to find out. I haven't had that many extraordinarily thrilling days lately. This sounds like something I can't afford to miss.

"Before we begin, I want you to turn to someone you don't know and introduce yourself," says the speaker. Since I have a history of being unwilling to participate even in audience clap-alongs at incredibly cool rock concerts, I am naturally planning to stare at my lap and pretend that I didn't hear the command when the woman seated in front of me turns, fixes me with a direct stare, offers me a hearty handshake, and tells me she is Barbara from Egghead Computer. That's when I remember I am a minority group member here—a spy in the ranks. I am the lone person from the customer sector.

"When we talk to a customer and they come up with an objection, it's a time of stress for us," says the speaker. "But remember, in our society customers are trained to automatically give objections. It's a time of stress for them, too."

This is a new one. The idea that my reluctance to throw out my own money on questionable purchases amounts to stress for salespeople has never occurred to me before. I usually regard salespeople as land mines in a ground war I would rather not fight. When I shop, I don't want to interact with anyone. I don't want to hear how nice I look. I don't want to hear how smart I am or what a wise decision I am making. But I never realized this made me a nightmare to all the people who now surround me here at SUCCESS 2000.

"In selling, it's not *what* you know but what you can *think of in time,*" the speaker tells us. He encourages us to open up our complimentary booklet ("Yes! You can learn how to sell effectively!") to page two and study the diagrammed hands that are labeled "The Precision Model." "Why do we use the precision model?" it asks on the bottom of the page. "Because PEOPLE NEVER SAY WHAT THEY MEAN."

"*All, every,* and *never* are 'universals,' " says the speaker. "They indicate a loop in the customer's mind. For example, a customer says to you, 'Everyone is buying Japanese cars.' You need to break that loop. So you respond, 'Everyone???' 'Well, I guess not *everyone,*' the customer is forced to admit. Now the loop is broken. Universals are *never* true." ("Never?" I want to yell out.) He's on a roll now. We're getting to the meat of the selling sandwich, so to speak. "Trying harder doesn't work," he tells us. "You know what works? The RMA works. What's the RMA? The Right Mental Attitude. And what feeds the RMA? The RPE. What's the RPE? Recent Positive Experiences."

The guy across the aisle from me blows his nose into a napkin and looks into it as Peter Lowe prepares to reveal the key: THE THREE RULES OF SELLING. He writes a single word on the overhead projector: Rapport. "Rapport. Rapport. Rapport. You *must* establish rapport with your customer," he explains. "How? Communicate based on their feelings. By matching someone's physiology exactly, by matching the tone of their speech, the volume of their speech, the tempo of their speech, you also build a rapport with them. And once you have a rapport, then you can shift into your sales pitch and they will shift with you."

This stuff is starting to make me uneasy. The very idea that there are books, tapes, whole schools of psychological and philosophical strategy designed to coerce me into buying things I don't necessarily want suddenly makes us customers sound like naïve victims in a big insidious plot. What recourse is there for the poor, overtaxed, underdefended customer? What schools of thought can we turn to in a brave attempt to hold our own in the face of such an onslaught? Which is why I now offer:

Obstinacy 2000. Yes, You Can Learn How to Buy Only What You Want To

1. The single greatest key to holding your own as a customer is NC: No Communication. To do this most effectively you will need to learn the perfect LMAF: The Leave Me Alone Face. You must appear to be a person whose every pore and follicle scream out, "I am a ticking time bomb. All my feelings are just about dead. Don't be the one to trigger the final frightening explosion."

2. If this is not immediately effective, remember that *salespeople never mean what they say.* So it will catch them off balance if you question the veracity of their every word. If the salesperson comments "You look very well in that outfit," respond instantly "Compared to what? To how I looked when I came into the shop? Are you saying you didn't like how I looked in what I was wearing when I came in?" They will answer, "No, no, I didn't mean that. I thought you looked very nice." "You did?" you reply. "I thought I looked horrible. Fat and bloated. If you thought *that* looked okay, I can't trust your judgment."

    All the while, be sure to Stand By *all* Your Universals (SBYU). For example, if you say "Everyone is buying Japanese cars," and the salesman says "Everyone?" you immediately snap, "Yes, *everyone*. Do you have some difficulty with your hearing? Maybe not everyone in the whole big wide world, but everyone that I know and have any respect for, which is all the people whose judgment matters to me. Now which other of my opinions do you want to pick apart and dispute, Mr. Waiting and Hoping and Praying for a Commission Sales Wizard?"

3. Meanwhile, be sure to watch closely to see if you are being "mirrored." When you lean forward, does your salesperson lean forward? When you speak softly, does he? If you sense that this is taking place, begin to behave erratically. Shout in the middle of a sentence. Sit down. Stand up. Spin around for no reason. Lie facedown on the counter and begin to sob quietly. Now take out the *Merck Manual* and insist that the salesperson help you to diagnose the symptoms that you feel. Does he think you have septicemia, liver tumors, or some kind of nerve damage? Do they have a sphygmomanometer on the premises? This is the moment when you must begin to overwhelm him with your HMA (Horrible Mental Attitude). Remind him of the futility of a frivolous materialistic purchase in a world so full of tragedies as ours. "Sure," you say, "I could start to make endless payments on this giganto TV, but wouldn't it be better if I just donated the whole sum to the United Nations International Children's Emergency Fund? Then at least I can write it off on my taxes. Not that I even have any money to spare." Now take out some of your current bills. "Look at this thirty-one-hundred-dollar Visa bill," you say. By now the salesperson should be wide-eyed, pale, and clammy; a twitching, throbbing, wretched mess. Which is precisely

the moment you choose to *close the deal*. "Do you like my watch?" you ask. "I got it as a Christmas present. It's a fif-teen-hundred-dollar value but I can let you have it for eight-fifty."

And before you know it, you will leave the store not only without a needless purchase but with pockets full of spending money you didn't expect to have when you came in! Plus the warm glow of satisfaction that comes from knowing you have avenged your fellow customers maybe for the first time ever.

Psychic
Comparison

Los Angeles offers its own special homegrown version of the Welcome Wagon. It comes in the form of a verbal gift basket of insider lists, delivered by a current resident to each and every newcomer. The list contains such useful tidbits as the names of street intersections where famous people got raped or killed, and the names of famous straight celebrities who are supposedly gay, and/or have been known to participate in vile and disgusting sexual practices, and/or have unusually large sexual organs. Thrown in as a bonus are several spa recommendations, tips on attending TV tapings, and the names of a couple of psychics.

Before I moved to L.A., I had never met anyone who had been to a psychic. But now, after living here for more than a decade, I can say unequivocally that every smart woman and gay male friend I currently have has been to at least a couple.

The urgent motivating force behind most of these psychic consultations tends to be love-related catastrophe. Although the core of the lunacy may well be the fact that most of my friends have no religious beliefs, so we all desperately want to pretend there is someone somewhere with a greater scope of vision who can provide us with access to magical solutions more profound than the ones we offer each other.

I am ashamed to admit that my own adventures in this dumb-girl realm have included a low point involving a middle-aged psychic with a henna rinse who replied to the questions "Do I have anything coming up work-wise?" with "I see something opening up for you in air-conditioning repair." "Gee," I remember saying, deeply disappointed by the direction my career was taking, "I don't really know anything about air conditioners. In fact, I'm not really very mechanical." "Well," she replied, unfazed, "I see where someone is going to take you on as an apprentice." Insane as this sounds, this was not the last money I paid to a psychic.

That is why I was not particularly surprised a couple of weeks ago when my good friend Susan, deep in the throes of romantic turmoil, called to report that she had just had an amazing psychic reading.

"She was phenomenal. Very detailed and specific," Susan gushed. "For example, she told me, 'You are with a man who loves you very much. He is a good man. But he is not the man for you.' " This rang such a bell with Susan that she went home and had the courage to finally break up with this guy.

"And you know what else she actually said to me? She said 'Who is Dan?' " Susan gasped. Dan was her previous boyfriend. "Then she said something really spooky. She said I would be going on three trips. 'I'm not worried about the first one. And I'm not worried about the third one,' she said. 'But the second one . . . don't get on a plane after eight at night.'

"You gotta go see her," Susan implored. "I am dying to hear what she tells you."

So I stored my sanity in a Ziploc bag where I hoped it would remain fresh, and drove out to the recesses of the San Fernando Valley, bearing the $80 I was willing to burn to hear a stranger's glorious vision of my happy future.

It did not seem like a good sign that there were two six-foot stuffed white teddy bears wearing crowns perched in the room where the reading was to occur. The psychic, a short-haired middle-aged woman with an unidentifiable Eastern European accent, told me to wait right outside on a couch by a gigantic scrapbook full of clipped and pasted magazine photos of famous actresses. Clients? I wondered. Or was she just the world's oldest obsessive teenage fan? Once the reading began, I found myself facing a wall full of eight-by-ten glossy headshots signed by many of these same extremely famous actresses.

The psychic shuffled the cards.

"I get 'D,' " she said to me. "Who is Dan?"

"My friend Susan's old boyfriend?" is what I did not say. "Something with a D," she continued, when Dan didn't ring any bells. "Don, maybe? David?"

I had a David, so I let her continue.

"There is a man in your life who loves you very much," she said to me. When I tried to counter with the information that there was no such man, she asked me not to interrupt. "He is a good man. But he is not really the man for you," she continued.

He is an invisible man, perhaps from another dimension, I thought. Lucky for him, or I might have to go home and break up with him.

"You are going to take three trips," she said. "I'm not worried about the first one. And I'm not worried about the third one. But the second one . . . well, my guides tell me that you should not fly after eight o'clock at night."

I guess I just witnessed an exhibition of classic Los Angeles girl questions and answers, I thought, searching desperately for a bright side while trying not to think of all the things I could have purchased for eighty bucks. *Well,* I thought as I got on the freeway, *at least I finally have concrete evidence that there are no psychics. Period. End of sentence.*

But just to be on the safe side, I thought, *if Susan invites me to fly somewhere with her, better make sure it's not her second trip.*

A New Closet
for Merrill

I believe the human race can be divided into two groups: those who gift-wrap neatly and those who don't. Those of us in the latter group understand that if we were to just slow down by a second or two, we could upgrade to the former. But for the same reason that we don't put things back on hangers with the top button buttoned, we can't seem to care enough to buy ourselves the extra second.

That is why, when last August a woman from *Good Morning America* asked me if it would be okay if the style editor from *Marie Claire* came to my house and organized my closet I said, without hesitation, "Absolutely." Of course, I felt a selfless urge to share the contents of my closet with a knowledge-hungry public. But mostly I was excited because these were the only plans to organize my closet that had been formulated since I stopped living with my parents several decades ago.

The day Mary Alice and her assistant, John, were introduced to my closet it was pretty much chaos in full bloom. The shelf at the top, which was loosely designated for sweaters and some pants, held a densely packed and crumpled heap of clothing the size and shape of an eight-year-old child. The hanging bar just below was so crowded that a crowbar was required to reinsert anything. And directly beneath that, on what would be the floor if you could see it, lay a hay-bale-shaped pile of shoes, some of which I hadn't laid eyes on since the Reagan administration.

Into this visual cacophony, carrying bundles of mysterious things, not unlike Santa and his helpers on Christmas Eve, stepped Mary Alice and John. Silently they went about their work.

First came a double layer of transparent cubicles across the top shelf, transforming it from an unapproachable wasteland to a planned community of tidy clothing condos, ready for occupancy. They color-coded my sweaters into piles so perfectly folded that I thought for a second I was living in the sportswear department at Neiman Marcus.

Next, the suit pants were wrenched from their hiding spots beneath suit jackets and relocated into a color-coded pants ghetto where Mary Alice now referred to them by the singular "pant." (As in, "That's a very good pant for you.") Each pant was uniformly hung by its waistband.

All the shirts were hung together. All the skirts were hung together. And all the clothes that were considered unacceptable for a woman with a closet like this one were put in a pile on my chair. For example, when Mary Alice saw my ankle-high cowboy boots with the low-slung buckle straps, circa 1988, she smiled at me patiently, like the exasperated mom of a demented child, then picked them up with one hand and hurled them across the room. I felt bad for them. Poor little boots. Once hot and sexy, now turned out by complete strangers like orphans on a cold winter night. Banished forever to a pile deemed too pathetic for the *new closet.*

And then—there it was: my intimidating new closet, looking like a department-store window that had been mysteriously inserted into my home. For the first time I had a closet that came with expectations I wasn't sure I could live up to. It could do better than me. I wasn't good enough for it. Suddenly it was I who was the interloper.

For quite a few days, I didn't go near the new closet at all. I would just quietly tiptoe past, so as not to offend its delicate sensibilities. It seemed like something I dare not touch with my bare hands, like some kind of a clothing museum. So I didn't take any clothes out. I didn't put any clothes in. I just left everything right where it was, fearful that I would introduce some new strain of bacteria into the fragile ecosystem. I also didn't touch any of the shamed and laughable discards that were quarantined in the throwaway pile in the corner.

Until, finally, there came a day when I needed to borrow a couple of clothes from my closet. Promising to bring them back in the condition in which I had borrowed them, I gingerly opened the closet and removed a pant and a shirt. On my best behavior, I carefully hung the pant back in Pant World and buttoned the top button on the blouse when I was finished borrowing them.

But as I continued to labor in this nerve-racking fashion, ever vigilant in my hanger placement and color coding, I realized something interesting. My old closet wasn't really gone. It was just in a dormant state, hiding inside my new closet, waiting for the right moment to poke its head through the way the Alien did from Sigourney Weaver's thorax.

It all began on the day that balancing my shoes on the specially designated shoe bars didn't go as well as I would have liked. One shoe fell behind, and I was too lazy to reach in carefully over the back of the other shoes to retrieve it.

Then the following day I was in too much of a hurry to put my jacket back in its appropriate neighborhood, since there was an empty space on the hanging bar right in front of me.

Later that evening I got up the courage to unfold a manically folded sweater from the pile of sweater origami designed by Mary Alice, but I lacked the manual dexterity to refold it so it matched the rest of the pile. I had asked Mary Alice for a folding lesson when I saw her work her magic, but by now her exacting technique was out of my grasp.

Once that had happened, the day when I put a black sweater on top of the blue pile wasn't very far behind. Soon there was a gold sweater living among the carefully folded blue jeans. And a red sweater on a hanger.

That was roughly the same time I corrupted everything else that was sacred by daring to reinsert my favorite items from the "banished forever" pile. Since then the decline has been steady, inevitable. It was always foretold. Nostradamus probably spoke of it.

The closet still looks a whole lot better than it did before Mary Alice and John worked their voodoo. But now I know the sad truth: We messy gift-wrappers *need* to have our shoes in a cantilevered pile. We like our closets messy. It is our way.

A Tenacious Grasp
of the Obvious

As a kind of a pointless brain teaser, I sometimes used to ponder what the irritating media equivalent of a televised sportscast for the non–sports fan might be . . . just in case I ever got a chance to inflict some sort of separate but equal revenge on an obsessed sports fanatic as retribution for the endless hours of sports broadcasts I have been made to endure over the years. What, if anything, I would ask myself, could possibly grate on their nerves the way the sound of droning play-by-play announcers intermixed with ambient crowd noises seems to grate on mine? And nothing seemed remotely hellish enough. Not the Weather Channel, not even Barney the Dinosaur . . . Until that sunny afternoon when I first encountered a home shopping show.

I immediately realized I had found the excruciating revenge I was seeking. Except for one fatal drawback. *I* wouldn't be able both to inflict it and stick around to revel in the results the way the sports fan can. Because home shopping is the only thing I have ever seen on TV that makes speedboat racing and afternoon golf seem not just watchable, but riveting and exciting by comparison.

Recently I heard fashion mogul Diane Von Furstenberg and media mogul Barry Diller conjecturing that they really couldn't visualize the TV owner who would not eventually be an eager home shopping participant. I suppose I ought to send them each my photo. I keep hearing that home shopping shows are popular, even addictive, but I don't understand how anyone can bear them. Starting with the stunning fact that they have finally succeeded in developing a category of television performer even more vile, superficial, and witless than the game-show host and the wacky weatherman combined.

I have heard it said more than once that these "shopping hosts" are like "family" to their regular viewers. And I can understand that, because in the real world the only circumstances under which I would tolerate this level of tedious empty-headed babbling are the occasions on which I have been trapped by tradition and politeness at various family functions.

There is a simple mathematical theorem that clearly explains my discomfort. A: the fact that I am someone who does not like to be talked to as though I were an idiot PLUS B: the fact that I also do not like to hear the opinion of salespeople when I am contemplating a purchase at a store PLUS C: the fact that these hosts seem to have been hired primarily for their ability to go on endlessly stating and restating the obvious in thousands of different ways until the product is all sold out EQUALS D: a video presentation as close to my own personal definition of "truly irritating" as I am anxious to get.

A portrait of one of these "hosts" written up in a Home Shopping Network publication called *The Bargaineer* listed among his qualifications "doing commercials for Toyota and Neutrogena Soap." "He thinks the best thing about the job," the article went on to say, "is the people calling in to talk. 'They're the real entertainment,' he says, 'they're the real stars.'"

Which brings us to the way in which home shopping has also succeeded in lessening the "minimum definition of entertainment"—a title that previously fell somewhere in between "calling a 900 number astrology forecast line" and "trying to get rid of the Jehovah's Witnesses on your porch." Not since Magic Johnson lost his late-night talk show has such boring, pointless conversation been available to such a wide audience.

If a guidebook exists to advise the novice shopping host, it must certainly contain the following conversational instructions: "No matter what a caller says to you, only one of two responses is ever necessary: 1. A gasp. 2. A laugh or chuckle."

Consider the following typical exchange from QVC:

Caller: Hi. This is Laurie from San Rafael.

Host: (Gasp) San Rafael! That's a great place to be from. Have you shopped with us before?

Caller: Yes. I have a couple of your weskits and I like them very much.

Host: (Chuckle) Oh! Those were a very good choice!

Caller: What I enjoy so much about them is that you can go casual or you can go formal.

Host: (Gasp) Very true! (Chuckle) Well, we're glad to have you back with us again today. (More chuckling)

Talk about real entertainment.

But conducting dozens of conversations that never rise above this level is only part of the job of the busy shopping host or hostess. The real meat of the job, so to speak, comes in endless hours of improvised sales pitches. There must have been a training seminar where they instructed these people to begin each pitch with an elaborate definition of even the commonest of products, followed by an endless listing of its possible uses, as though the whole thing were being viewed by someone completely new to our galaxy who might not have even the most rudimentary grasp of any of our concepts.

"It's a polished silver picture frame," I heard one guy begin his pitch on QVC, "great for any picture you might have. It's perfect for those wedding photos or maybe you have some photos of your recent vacation—this is ideal, or perhaps some photos of someone who just graduated—this would be wonderful. Or how about snapshots of the new grandchild? Or shots from the big office party . . . ?" He was just getting started.

"This is my first ruby ring," I heard Charlene of *Shopping with Charlene* on the Home Shopping Network say. "Deep dark *vivacious* [sic] rubies. And whether this is going to be your first ruby red ring or perhaps your tenth or your sixth or you're looking for something for the lady in your life or maybe adding to your collection . . ." *Help!* Somebody make these people stop before I go down there and do things I'm certain to regret!

Which brings us to the lingo. The language choices on home shopping shows are so full of newly minted terms for things of questionable pedigree that it amounts to the sales equivalent of a Napoleon complex. *Every* piece of jewelry has a glamorous-sounding official name. What looks like a diamond on HSN is called "cubic zirconium." It's known as "Diamonique" on QVC. A recent viewing of the *Discover Dia-*

monique show on QVC featured "simulated emeralds" ("It puts the true emerald to shame. It's such a lovely shade of dark green"), "Caribbean Ice," and "Lilac Ice, which some people call simulated tanzanite" ("It goes with everything. A gorgeous ring. Just perfect"). Other pieces were "designer inspired" and laden with "faux pearls," then "gold layered by techni-bond." And all of these expensive-sounding terms go drifting by, unremarked upon, as though they might actually mean something. Certain things also come with "a certificate of authenticity."

They are all part of a universe of theoretically prestigious references that seem to exist only within the boundaries of home shopping channels. This also includes "Capodimonte figurines" and "Kanchanaburi sapphires." ("Have you bought Kanchanaburi sapphires with us before?" asks Charlene. "Oh yes," says a caller. "I've got so many rings I don't know where to put them.")

And then there are the celebrity product lines. A few years ago the big name was Farrah Fawcett, who was hawking her "exclusive line of jewelry" based on "replicas of pieces she wore in movies" and "reproductions of jewelry given to her by Ryan O'Neal." I thought that was the most touching idea I'd ever heard of—turning the personal tokens of love you received from your boyfriend into a line of inexpensive jewelry for the mass market—but that was before I saw Joan Rivers on QVC just the other night selling her "pearl clasp expandable bracelet." "Fabulous! Fabulous! So elegant! So chic!" she said, explaining that it was a duplicate of a piece given to her by her late husband, Edgar Rosenberg, who we all know took his own life. Talk about a sentimental gesture! Talk about a fool for love! Joan was also offering "the Joan Rivers pavé crystal earrings—a gift from Robert Goulet." I guess the smart person should sign a contract with her before attending any holiday function where presents are exchanged.

I realize that millions of happy, satisfied viewers do not seem to be as repelled by this stuff as I am. Repelled, nothing. The fanatical love they feel is palpable. "You know, Cathy, I heard you three years ago when you talked to a lady from Oakland during the big fire," I heard a QVC caller say, "and she said she had to get off. She was being evacuated." "Yes, I remember," said the host, Cathy. "You made the *San Francisco Chronicle*," the caller went on. "Her house burned down." "I know," said Cathy. "Some of our fabulous viewers sent me the article. She wrote us a follow-up letter and said she couldn't believe she was shopping at a time like that. She said she really is a rational woman and is getting her life back together." Then she went on to sell the caller a simulated emerald "with a touch of hugs and kisses on the side. The perfect ring."

It's pretty apparent that, with or without my approval, home shopping is on the rise. It does combine two national obsessions—the love of spending and the love of television.

But as for me, the only thing I personally stand to gain from its presence is that now there is programming I find so thoroughly irritating I may finally have found a motive for becoming a sports fan.

Things to Do While Waiting for the World to End

Many people believe the end of the world is coming very soon. But whether or not you socialize with seemingly normal people who forward you Nostradamus quotes on e-mail, as I do, there is really no downside to putting your life in order. As with Christmas, you don't want to leave it all to the last minute. But where to start? Here are my suggestions.

Revise Your Life Goals

Understand That Some Things Will Always Be Unknowable.

You will not have the answers in this lifetime to such questions as "Why was Adam Sandler such a huge success?" Or "Why did everybody love Raymond?" Or "What exactly was the big deal with Ryan Seacrest, anyway?"

Accept That You Will Not Accomplish
All the Goals You Set for Yourself.

For example, it is probably too late now to become "a Beltway insider" or even find out what one is. Ditto for those big household projects you've been putting off. The end of the world is not a good time to begin refinishing your floors.

Focus on the Achievable.

Stop lying to yourself. Don't say you're going to read *War and Peace* or that book by Stephen Hawking when you know damn well that even when facing the end of the world, all you are really going to do is fall asleep reading and rereading page one.

Put together a realistic reading list. You can tackle a few long literary masterpieces or a stunning quantity of short popular paperbacks. Bear in mind that if the world starts up again, it will sound more impressive when you say you used the End Times to read hundreds of books. Considering the stress everyone attending the end of the world will be under, no one is going to ask you to list the books by their titles. That's why it's a good idea to stock up on as many tawdry crime novels, celebrity tell-alls, and assorted volumes of semiliterate smut as you can get your hands on.

Diet

Stop Trying to Lose Weight.

Go ahead and get really fat. Now. The worst thing that can happen is you will die of a heart attack or a stroke, and relatively speaking, that's really not the end of the world. No use pondering whether chromium picolinate really does speed up the metabolism. You probably won't even have an appetite after the anthrax hits. Stock up on plenty of cocktail peanuts and margarita mix—we are never going to get a definitive answer as to whether alcohol is good or bad for us, so you might as well drink to excess.

The same logic, of course, could be used as a reason to start a heroin habit. But only if you can buy such an enormous quantity from a non-Taliban source that you are sure you will not run out. The end of the world will be traumatic enough without having to simultaneously search for a rehab center.

Wardrobe

After the end of the world, fashion will be at a standstill. So there is no time like the present to begin cultivating the look you would like to have for the Apocalypse. Think practical: Platform shoes, transparent fabrics, or anything by Prada are not good Armageddon choices. Instead, plan on a colorful layered look that will not only boost your spirits but also hold up under a variety of wacky weather conditions.

Sex

Remember, ladies, it's finally okay to have sex without thought of commitment since a commitment can't really be long-term anymore. But choose your indiscriminate liaisons wisely. If there's not much time left, then it makes sense to only have sex with people who know what they are doing. Focus on commitment-phobic sociopathic types who have been working this angle for years: Musicians are still a good bet, but you may find that congressmen, prisoners out on parole, and show business executives will be even more in demand than usual.

Priorities

As we approach the end of the world, it becomes officially okay to abandon certain antiquated behaviors. For instance, forget about:

- rewinding Blockbuster films
- wiping the backs of shelves
- watching MTV video roundups to stay current
- knowing the names of the newest Survivors
- keeping an eye on the gardeners
- maintaining your Christmas card list
- staying up-to-date on insurance payments
- saving those fucking *New York Times Book Review*s

Also: FIRE THE SHRINK. As the end draws near, many kinds of mental illnesses and neuroses will be regarded as sensible behavioral choices. And now is the time to confront your weirdest obsessions. For instance, have you always wondered what it would feel like to pound your fist into the center of a chocolate mousse cake?

Maybe I've said too much.

Zombie Clerks
Are Messing
with My Mind

I am not averse to a certain amount of pointless cheery chit-chat. I talk to friends and animal companions alike about nothing of real importance on a regular basis. I also exchange pleasantries with strangers on checkout lines, and goof around with waiters and waitresses in restaurants whenever the mood strikes me.

At least, I *used* to do these things. Until it came to my attention that a new level of increased friendliness I had been noticing on the part of employees of large chain stores was the result of elaborate instructions from management on the art of how to manipulate me. And not just me (although the thought of being singled out by national chains as special has a certain appeal). No, you're included in this, too.

There's something aggressively soulless and robotic going on in the world of commerce and chitchat. Ever since I became aware of it, I feel a little like the central character in the movie *Invasion of the Body Snatchers*.

It all began when I started to notice that the various women running the cash registers at my neighborhood market seemed unusually interested in the contents of my purchase. At first, I thought that perhaps I had stumbled on one of my lesser-known talents. Apparently I was a more-fascinating-than-average shopper. "No one really picks out the half-sour pickle slices and the mock chicken patties made of soy protein like I do," I said to myself, chuckling, as the checkout women gushed, making comments like "This looks really interesting" or "I bet this is delicious!" "Well, I'm trying it for the first time, but I'll let you know," I would reply proudly, still a little puzzled by all the attention but imagining that they might be trying to decide if they had the personal courage to join me in this brave new world of adventurous product tasting that I was pioneering.

Meanwhile, I was secretly thinking, *It's amazing that after so many years of working at this market, these women are still able to be* riveted *by what is for sale here since you'd think they must have rung up* everything in the store *fifty billion times. . . . Perhaps they are simple people,* I finally concluded, *which is probably kind of a blessing since it helps them survive the tedium of an otherwise thankless, repetitive job.*

That was before I discussed this very topic with a friend who worked the cash register at a similar kind of market. He told me about the training video his market manager made the employees watch. In it, through a series of unintentionally hilarious scenarios performed by uniquely wooden actors, the store employees were given specific instructions on how to perform the very bits of friendly interest in a customer's selections that I had been pondering. "Once I made the commitment to *force myself* to say hello and talk to everyone, I found out that *it was fun!!*" a reluctant "employee" testified on tape.

Not long after, I got ahold of a copy of "Communicating Coffee," the sixty-four-page training manual for employees of a large coffee franchise with a name kind of like "Barstucks." There it all was again. Page after page of specific instructions on how to make customers think you actually enjoyed seeing them come in the door and talking to them. "Connect with customers within 30 seconds by welcoming them, and establishing a relationship," it said. "Ask questions about their personal coffee consumption habits. Make recommendations to identify how you can help."

Later that same day, I found myself shopping at a big, popular sportswear franchise. But now, when I noticed an unusually high level of interactive chitchat taking place at the cash register, I heard a horror movie sting in my head. Goose bumps crept over me. Here were more people *forcing themselves* to talk cheerily to me and pretend that they cared about me as a person. When the blond sales-surfer looked up from folding the blouse I was about to buy and said, "It's a beautiful day out. Do you have some fun plans for the weekend?" I had to fight the urge to turn and run out to the parking lot screaming, "They already got to these people, too! Quick! Everyone! Run for your lives!"

Because I am the kind of shopper who doesn't want a salesman hovering around me, asking if I need any help, or a saleswoman volunteering any unsolicited lies about how great I look in the clothes I am trying on, I find this whole fake conversational thing to be a complete nightmare. It scares me to think that possibly everyone I run into on a daily basis in the world of commerce has been programmed like a live human version of an automated message.

I never thought that anything would make me nostalgic

for the days of snotty, ill-tempered, IQ-impaired slacker retail clerks and hostile waitresses, but this big new world of cheery, fake, forced conversation is causing those feelings to surface. It's all the more frightening to me because over the years, I have come to the conclusion that excessive job cheeriness equals incompetence. Real competence in any job tends to make a person grouchy.

Which is not to say that I want to go back to the day of arrogant, muttering zombies. Although, looking back, I see that the irritation they were serving up at least reflected some amount of backbone and connection to reality. It also didn't require any energetic false-positive behavior in return from me.

But it's too late. This trend is creeping subtly through job populations you'd never imagine it would touch, just the way the aliens in *Invasion of the Body Snatchers* did. "They just brought in a customer-relations specialist at our museum," my brother, an art curator, told me. "We're all going to have to attend seminars about how to approach the public."

The weirdest thing is that now that I know that this genial talk is mandatory, it makes me, in my role as the customer, want to return every suspiciously friendly conversational foray with a stern glance and a one-word answer. Simply because it's the only response unmanipulated by customer-relations automatons that is still left open. "Try and chat me up, asshole," I want to say. "*You* have to pretend you want to talk to me, but I don't have to pretend I want to answer." Maybe spontaneous human interactions in the workplace are going to become relics of a bygone era. But, if I have my way, the days of the really, really irascible, totally unprogrammed customer are only just beginning.

What I Did on My Summer Vacation

Perusing the things-to-do section of the newspaper, I was taken by a little drawing of happy cows riding on a roller coaster. "Don't miss *your* San Fernando Fair," it said. "We're on the Mooove." If *cows* could enjoy the damn thing, I reasoned, so could I. And I was on my way until I saw the ad directly below it. FREE SCREEN TEST. ACT IN MOTION PICTURES, TV. BEGINNERS WANTED—WE TRAIN. Why not, for God's sake? This is L.A.!

So I find myself walking into a storefront. Just across from a mortuary, on a Hollywood street. Inside, the receptionist, a fiftyish woman with dark, pinned-up hair, motions for me to sit on a couch flanked by two plastic palm trees. The room is heavily decorated with paintings of Elvis and a few eight-by-ten glossies of women in swimwear and high heels shaking hands with men, none of whom I can identify. The receptionist is talking to a big, good-looking guy in his thirties about how she used to dance professionally with Mario Lanza when a young black woman with dreadlocks is ushered out of an inner office and I am instructed to go in.

Inside, a stocky white-haired man is seated at a desk. "My, what a pretty girl you are," he says to me. "Do you think you could handle leading parts in pictures?" Immediately I am impressed by his good taste and judgment. "We're a studio," he tells me. "We just make one picture after another. We've been here since 1938. I'm eighty-one years old. I've been directing and producing since I was seventeen. You could do commercials." Then he tells me, "You're a young stewardess type. Would you like to earn $1,000 to $1,200 a week?" "Well, okay," I say, adjusting immediately to my new role as media whore.

"It's a government school," he tells me. "The whole course is six hundred dollars, but the government pays the whole thing. It's called grants." "I don't get it," I tell him. "Doing a commercial is paid for by a government grant?" I ask about the screen test. "That's just for beginners," he says. "Why don't I have you try out for speaking parts? I can see you're ready to work. I want you to read this skit with that young man out there." Then he hands me a three-page scene from something called *Saturday's Children*, written for two characters named Bobby and Rims. "What can you tell me about the character I'm playing?" I ask. "Her name is Bobby. She's a woman," he says as he shows me into a dilapidated back room full of motel-art-type paintings. The big, good-looking guy is already back there. "You two read this together. Then I'll be back to take a look at you," he tells us.

So we begin to rehearse the scene, which sounds as if it was written in the thirties because of its oddly dated turns of phrase, such as, "Oh, Rims, dear, don't you get tired of poor me? Ever?" My scene partner, although clearly all-American, reads English as though it is his second language. Even after six rehearsals, our scene still falls short of what you might call entertainment. Suddenly the receptionist bursts in. "It's eventually all going back to radio," she tells us firmly. "It *has* to. In TV everyone has to be so glamorous, but in radio you can show up with your hair in curlers. Although I wouldn't advise it because sometimes there *is* a small audience."

Now she hands us another scene to read. It's called *Wilderness Wife*. "In the wilderness of northern Ontario stands a little log cabin," my partner, who is now the narrator, reads in a voice that sounds like he's coming out of a heavy anesthesia. "And inside, Myra Webster is making some meat pies. Way off in the distance a man plobs his way toward the cabin."

"Plows," the receptionist corrects him. "I made a mistake when I typed this."

"When he reaches her side, he drops a bundle of beaver pelts, puts his arm around her and kisses her," the narrator continues, and begins to move toward me. "You don't have to touch," the receptionist interjects. "*Real* actors can get their point across without ever touching anyone." Before we can get our point across she suggests that we accompany her backstage. "I'd like to show you a few things," she says, as I think I hear the theme from *The Twilight Zone*. "Usually I work for Rockwell on the B-1 bomber," the big guy enthuses as we return to a stage area that is decorated with a green Naugahyde couch and two little paintings of pixies. "Now I want each of you to get up onstage and say why you want to be an actor," she says. Lucky for me the big guy gets right up.

"The reason I want to be an actor is that it seems like an interesting field," he says. "Okay, now do a little scene," the receptionist tells him. "Act something out." The big guy pauses, turns his profile to us, and addresses two imaginary people. "I think you've both had enough to drink," he says, "and now I'm going to have to ask you to leave." Turning back to us, he explains, "I used to be a bouncer." "Very good!" says the receptionist, spearheading the applause. It's been two hours and I still have no idea where this is leading, so I mention that I have another appointment. "Well, please talk to the director on your way out," the receptionist instructs me, turning all her attention to the big guy.

The "director" is sitting alone in his office, hidden behind piles of paper on his desk. "I didn't realize you were such a dynamic actress," he says to me. "You could sell anything. Phone sales. You ever do that?" "No," I say, frankly crushed that I have been demoted from leading lady to telephone salesperson in no time at all. "Well, I'm going to get you some work," he promises me. "You'd be perfect for a show like *L.A. Law*. And I think I have a picture for you." "What kind of picture?" I ask him. "Super 8," he says. "Can you be reached evenings after seven?" I tell him I can. "I was also interested in that big boy out there," he says to me. "How's he doing?" "Well," I say, "he's fine. Except he doesn't have any idea of how to read lines." "*L.A. Law,*" the guy says to me. "I'm gonna get him on *L.A. Law*." And I never heard from any of them again.

Top Dog

Recently I received an odd letter in the mail. It was printed on stationery headed "Who's Who in Canine America, LTD." I couldn't tell if it was a standard form letter or one from someone familiar with my legendary (some say "magical and transcendent," others "neurotic and repulsive") rapport with dogs.

"Dear Merrill Markoe," it said. "Our dogs make paw prints on our hearts. They are more lovable and charming than any other creatures on earth."

Certainly fighting words to new mothers, fans of *NSYNC, and anyone who watches more than an hour a week of Pokémon. But I digress.

"This is what Who's Who in Canine America is all about," the letter went on. "Yes, we want your dog to be included in this first and only volume. This is an honor offered to less than one percent of all dogs and their owners in America."

Hmmm. My interest was building. The idea of joining this elite cadre was now helping me step past the bitterness I felt at the fact that my dogs had accrued "Who's Who" credibility and honors while I, as a human, went unacknowledged.

"There is no cost or obligation to be selected for this wonderful treasury," the letter explained. "Please make sure your dog is included by completing and returning the enclosed Acceptance and Reservation form today."

This was followed by a place to enter your seven-digit credit card number so you could be billed for the $49.95 plus $4.95 shipping and handling per volume. No cost or obligation at all. Just the slightly suspicious price per volume of fifty-five bucks.

But there was another more troubling set of issues with which to deal. I have four dogs, each spectacular in his own way. Repeated readings of the aforementioned solicitation revealed no way that more than one dog per household could possibly be nominated.

Why? Because it would make this incredible tome too long? Surely it couldn't be because "Who's Who in Canine America" couldn't figure out a way to sell a separate fifty-five-dollar volume for each additional dog?

Whatever the reason, now I was facing my own version of Sophie's choice. Which of my four dogs was going to be immortalized? The "anything you would like to add about this very special family member" section of the application would have to provide the criteria.

Typically animals are singled out for acclaim because of their abilities to rescue humans. Newspapers regularly sing the praises of dogs who pull owners from turbulent waters, or wake them so they can escape from a fire.

But in my opinion, standard-issue heroic animal gestures are predictable, unrealistic, and irrelevant. Each of my dogs' distinguishing abilities were more subtle, more specific and so-phisticated than those lifeguarding, drug-sniffing, Seeing Eye showboats who always hog all the praise.

Take, for example, my dog Winky, an abandoned Shih Tzu whom I found six years ago when he was enough of a cool-headed adventurer to be taking a hike along the soft shoulder of a busy highway. Right from the beginning I could see he ex-hibited what can only be considered an inspirational degree of enthusiasm for the consumption of food. So exuberant are his feelings, so hot and keen his passion, so rapt his attention that every single day during meal preparation he dances backward, like an outfielder trying to catch a fly ball, into the same water dish in order to maintain a fixed and steady gaze when his bowl begins to make the journey from the kitchen countertop to the floor. Then, once the inhaling of breakfast is over, some three to five seconds later, Winky continues to exhibit vigi-lance beyond the call of duty by proceeding, without instruc-tion or encouragement, to help rid the cooking area of debris and microorganisms by licking the entire surface of the kitchen floor. This impressive effort is a testament not just to his tenacity and his spirit but to his creativity, ingenuity, and limitless heart as well.

Then there is Tex, a medium-size brown-and-black dog of indeterminate origin whose deceptively simpleminded facial expressions mask the important life lessons he has to teach re-garding the nature of problem solving. For example, when left behind in the house with the front door locked and all the windows closed, Tex does not see limitations, only possibili-ties. Could he make an exit through the bookshelf, once the books are removed, by chewing through the living room wall? How about expanding the definition of "door" by removing the superfluous wooden frame? Sure, these are tasks that a lesser dog might find daunting. But not Tex.

Yet, once he successfully breaks through to the other side of whatever it is he has conquered, does he run around gloating in his triumph? No. He stands, perturbed, ill at ease, unsure of what to do now, seemingly preoccupied with finding a route back into the house. A wasted effort? No. He is simply trying to impart a valuable lesson: The accomplishment of a goal is not a destination so much as it is another starting place. Like any good Zen master, he has given me something to contemplate to facilitate my growth as a sentient being.

Finally, there is Lewis, my hundred-pound black dog, sent to teach the power of unconditional love. And what better continuous example than the way he conducts his long-term relationship with my sofa. Each day, when the house is cleaned and the throw pillows are nicely arranged along the top, Lewis is seduced anew as though the sofa were adorned in provocative lingerie. And yet, once the slipcovers are filthy, the throw pillows scattered, and the sofa looking old and broken, worn and infirm, Lewis looks past the superficial and remains as full of desire as ever. Who among us does not aspire to a love so deep and abiding?

And so we see that each dog is such an exemplary specimen it is all but impossible to choose. Should it be Winky, Tex, or Lewis in the "Who's Who"? Maybe it should be the one who's willing to kick in his share of the fifty-five bucks.

A Full-Disclosure Candidacy

As we draw ever closer to another national election, we find ourselves in the rare position of being able to observe the birth of a new political tradition. I am referring to the soon to be mandatory use of what is sometimes called inoculation—going public with the confession of some private foible before your political opponent or the press can use it to drag your name through the mud.

Recent examples of this are everywhere: George W. Bush bothering to admit that he enjoyed a wild extended youth as pundits continue to encourage him to come clean about his use of cocaine; Senator John McCain of Arizona feeling the need to mention that he strayed in his first marriage; Clint Reilly, a Democrat running for mayor of San Francisco, making a thirty-second television commercial in which he looked into the camera and confessed, "Twenty years ago I had a drinking problem."

Even across the Atlantic in jolly old England, a guy named Michael Portillo, vying for leadership of Britain's Conservative party, shocked the local political establishment not too long ago by announcing that he had had homosexual experiences in college.

Clearly, full personal disclosure is the wave of the future. Whether this turns out to be good or bad remains to be seen. But I believe that one day soon, all new statements of candidacy will sound approximately like this.

Fellow citizens and respected members of my party: Although I have not been much of a hat wearer in recent years, I would like at this time to throw my hat into the ring. I have the vision, the dedication, the energy, and the innovative ideas needed to lead our country in the twenty-first century.

But before I share some of the exciting programs I am planning, there are a few things about me I feel you should know.

In the seventh grade I was caught looking at the answers to a history test, which I had written on the bottom of my shoe. This was a very rebellious time in my life, during which I received numerous hours of after-school detention for talking without raising my hand and making fart noises using my armpit. I regret this behavior and have continued to compensate for it by doing a great deal of supplementary reading about the War of 1812.

Everyone knows that the teen years can be a behavioral mine field, which is the only explanation I can offer as to why I attended several parties with a group of underage friends who consumed large quantities of a certain brand of cough syrup that contained a lot of alcohol. In a misguided attempt to form an educated opinion, I tried but ultimately rejected marijuana, cocaine, and diet pills, settling finally on a light diet of what the kids called magic mushrooms even though I was aware that they were neither magic nor even in the mushroom family. These experiences were regrettable and I have not consumed any drugs at all since my junior year in college.

However, my senior year, adrift in the overwhelming stress of upcoming law school entrance exams, I experienced an uncharacteristic period of moral confusion during which I was persuaded, against my better judgment, by a girl with whom I was having a very turbulent, short-lived relationship, to participate in what was then called a three-way. Connected to this was an unfortunate incident involving the transmission of a type of body louse (with which I was temporarily infested) to a rather large number of my immediate peers.

In this same period, I regret to admit, I was not entirely frank with quite a number of girls, to whom I professed false feelings of love to gain sexual favors. On several occasions I invited them to dine with me in expensive restaurants and then when the check arrived pretended to have forgotten my wallet, thus causing them to have to pay for my dinner. At the end of the evening I would always assure them that I would call them soon, knowing full well that I never would.

I can't change my past. But I do continue to strive each day to be the best person I can be. I am pleased to announce that this past year I totally eliminated my tendency to speed through yellow lights at the very last second, an unfortunate habit that was at the root of my many moving-violation citations. I have also given my word to the people with whom I work that I will correct what they call my pattern of giving inappropriately cheap seasonal gifts, and will stop claiming that I am going to the gym when I am actually just heading home early to nap. In coming months, I plan to openly admit that the reason I did not lose weight after three months on the Zone was not a glandular disorder but the fact that I keep a stash of Snickers and Hershey's Kisses behind the corporate checkbook in the bottom drawer of my desk.

Yes, I regret the things I did. But I also embrace them for helping to make me the honorable, law-abiding, churchgoing citizen and monogamous family man that I am today. As most of you know, I have been happily married to my lovely wife, Lana, for eleven of the fourteen years we have been together, and faithful to her for almost three.

Acknowledgments

Thanks to Bruce Tracy, Melanie Jackson, and Marty Tenney, for getting this republished; Polly Draper, Michael Wolff, Robin McCarthy, and Susan Jaffee, for going along on stuff; Dawn Mazzella and Hallie, Dean Graulich, and the staff of the Pacific Coast Animal Hospital.

Also, thanks to Bob, Stan, Lewis, Bo, Tex, Winky, Puppyboy, and Dink, for providing me with content, and Andy Prieboy for everything else.

About the Author

Five-time Emmy Award–winning writer MERRILL MARKOE has published three books of humorous essays and the novels *The Psycho Ex Game* (with Andy Prieboy) and *It's My F---ing Birthday.* She has worked as a radio host and a TV correspondent and written for television, movies, and a delightful assortment of publications. She lives in Los Angeles, if you can call that living.

About the Type

This book was set in Garamond, a typeface originally designed by the Parisian typecutter Claude Garamond (1480–1561). This version of Garamond was modeled on a 1592 specimen sheet from the Egenolff-Berner foundry, which was produced from types assumed to have been brought to Frankfurt by the punchcutter Jacques Sabon.

Claude Garamond's distinguished romans and italics first appeared in *Opera Ciceronis* in 1543–44. The Garamond types are clear, open, and elegant.